TORNADO
21st CENTURY STEAM

Jonathan Glancey

'The definitive work...'
The A1 Steam Locomotive Trust

BOOKS ON TRACK WWW.BOOKSONTRACK.CO.UK

ACKNOWLEDGEMENTS

The author would like to thank the following for their help in bringing this book up to full working pressure: Mark Allatt, Chris Bayliss, Eddie Bobrowski, Graeme Bunker, George Carpenter, David Champion, Phil Champion, Don Clarke, David Elliott, Malcolm Crawley, Sue Graves, Gerard Hill, Danny Hopkins, Matt Howell, Howard Johnston, Matt Johnston, Simon Johnston, Tommy Knox, Jon Longman, Dorothy Mather, Phil Metcalfe, Gavin Morrison, Mike Notley, Rob Morland, Jon Pridmore, Geoff Rixon, Jim Smith, Brian Stephenson, Tony Streeter, Alexa Stott, Peter Townend, Neil Whitaker and Barry Wilson. Wider thanks are due, of course, to the A1 Steam Locomotive Trust and to everyone who made Tornado possible.

First published in October 2010 by Books On Track
Eaglethorpe Barns, Warmington, Northamptonshire, PE8 6TJ UK
Tel: +44 (0)1832 281130
Fax: +44 (0)1832 281145
www.booksontrack.co.uk

Copyright © Books On Track 2010

Designed by Sherbert Design
Printed by Butler, Tanner & Dennis, UK
ISBN 978-0-9566770-0-6

CARING FOR THE ENVIRONMENT

This book was printed in the UK by Butler, Tanner & Dennis, saving the environmental cost of long-distance transportation to major markets. The printing facility has all its operations under one roof and employs mainly local people, many cycling to work. It is certified ISO 1400. It was printed using 100% vegetable-based inks on Condat Matt FSC paper. Condat Matt FSC is produced from 100% Elemental Chlorine Free (EFC) pulp that is fully recyclable. It has a Forest Stewardship Council (FSC) accreditation and is produced by a mill which supports well-managed forestry schemes.

FSC
Mixed Sources
Product group from well-managed forests, controlled sources and recycled wood or fibre

Cert no. SGS-COC-005091
www.fsc.org
©1996 Forest Stewardship Council

TORNADO
21st CENTURY STEAM

Jonathan Glancey

BOOKS ON TRACK WWW.BOOKSONTRACK.CO.UK

A crowning moment for No. 60163 at York station on 19th February 2009. The locomotive is about to be formally named *Tornado* by their Royal Highnesses Prince Charles and the Duchess of Cornwall. They are joined by A1 Steam Locomotive Trust Chairman Mark Allatt.

NEIL WHITAKER/A1 STEAM LOCOMOTIVE TRUST

"I greatly enjoyed my ride on the footplate…"

HRH The Prince of Wales accepted the invitation to officially name *Tornado* (with the Duchess of Cornwall) in February 2009, and little over a year later rode on No. 60163's footplate on an outing to Manchester. He wrote this heartfelt letter to the A1 Steam Locomotive Trust, thanking the team for the memorable experience:

Dear Mr Allatt

I did just want to send my warmest thanks to you and your colleagues at the A1 Steam Locomotive Trust for once again providing such marvellous support during my visit to Manchester the other day.

It was wonderfully appropriate to use the Tornado locomotive to arrive at the Museum of Science and Industry and, needless to say, I greatly enjoyed my ride on the footplate late in the day. Please do thank Inspector Gareth Jones, Driver Bob Hart, Fireman Frank Sutton and Graeme Bunker, who all helped to make the journey a most memorable experience. I was covered in soot at the end of the journey..!

This comes with my warmest good wishes and heartfelt thanks – together with the hope that there will be other opportunities to deploy the Tornado on future Royal Train expeditions.

Yours most sincerely

Charles

Tornado, Britain's newest main line express steam locomotive has taken 18 years and £3 million to bring to life.

MATT HOWELL

CONTENTS

FOREWORD

Recreating lost designs of steam locomotives seems to have become a British national pastime, but from the many proposed projects from the mid-1980s (I counted 26 at one point), only a few have started construction, and all are many years behind No. 60163 *Tornado* in terms of completion.

I've often been asked why I got involved in the project. After all, I wasn't born until the end of 1965, so am far too young to remember an 'A1' in a scrapyard, let alone in action. A photograph of me taken at an open day at Barrow Hill depot in 1971 shows my first encounter with a Peppercorn Pacific, 'A2' No. 532 *Blue Peter*. Although I was only five years old, the experience left a lasting impression on me.

Peppercorn's 49 'A1s' were the last great express passenger locomotives designed by the London & North Eastern Railway, but built by British Railways at Doncaster and Darlington in 1948/49. At the front of luxury Pullman trains from London to Yorkshire and the North East, they were the last word in post-war speed, style and glamour – yet quickly discarded when diesels came along.

The final Peppercorn 'A1' was tragically scrapped in 1966, and 24 years later a project began to build a new one, No. 60163 *Tornado*, which made her debut in August 2008.

She is truly a 'Royal' engine, because she was officially named by their HRHs The Prince of Wales and Duchess of Cornwall at York station on 19th February 2009, and she subsequently starred in the BBC TV programme *Top Gear*, when seven million people saw a black-faced Jeremy Clarkson on her footplate shovelling coal.

Jonathan Glancey is uniquely qualified to write this book as he has been following the *Tornado* story since the mid-1990s and has reported every twist and turn on the way. This book tells the story of the 'A1s' and the extraordinary *Tornado* project, its highs and its lows, and of some of the people whose shared vision and determination to bring what many said was just a pipedream to life.

I believe that the Trust's success is largely due to adhering to a few simple principles right from the start. Thanks to thousands of supporters and backing form the best of British business (our principal sponsor is William Cook Cast Products) we have raised the £3 million needed. Even so, we still need to repay the outstanding £500,000 borrowed to complete construction and you can still come on board by either becoming a regular donor, making a one-off payment, sponsoring a component, or taking a 'slice' of *Tornado's* new support coach. Help us to keep steam alive by ensuring that *Tornado* has a great future where she belongs – on the main line.

Mark Allatt
Chairman
A1 Steam Locomotive Trust

CHAPTER ONE

Setting the scene
The mechanical
supermodel

The arctic winters of 1962–63 and 1946–47 had been colder, bitter even, in an age when few homes boasted central heating and instant hot water. And, yet for anyone under the age of 30, the winter of 2009–10 was the snowiest they could possibly remember. The extremities of Britain froze. Kent, in particular, became a winter wonderland for those with a childlike gleam in their eyes, but a significant worry for those trying to keep the county on the move. By 21st December, the struggle had become all too much for modern day electric commuter trains; they all but ground to a halt.

Very few trains ran in Kent that day. One that had no problem was the 'Cathedrals Express'. Why? Because, this heavy, 13-coach train was hauled from Victoria to Canterbury and Folkestone, and back, during the day and again during the evening by locomotive No. 60163 *Tornado*. *Tornado* is, of course, a steam locomotive, and a very special one indeed. The first brand new main line steam locomotive built in Britain since 1960, she [traditionally, steam locomotives have always been female, even when named after men] made her public debut in November 2008 and proved, instantly, wholly competent and hugely popular.

In her first full year of operation, *Tornado* made many friends, winning admirers and a place in the nation's imagination and media. The 'Cathedrals Express' received congratulatory press coverage on 22nd December. That morning, *Tornado's* exploits were aired on BBC Radio 4's Today programme. A clearly chuffed John Humphrys

Right: The big freeze of winter 1963 put many replacement diesels out of action, and provided steam with its last great chance to show what it could do. 'A1' No. 60117 *Bois Roussel* is at Markham near Doncaster with an up express.
DEREK PENNEY

Below: Yet 47 years on, about the only train running to time when bad weather hit the South East on 21st December 2009 was the steam-hauled 'Cathedrals Express'. No. 60163 passes Staplehurst… and some of its passengers are thankful commuters left stranded because their electric trains have broken down.
CRAIG STRETTON/A1 STEAM LOCOMOTIVE TRUST

'A1' No. 60163 *Tornado* stands at London's Victoria station with the 'Cathedrals Express.' Due to bad snow affecting electric services, *Tornado* came to the rescue of stranded commuters that evening, 21st December 2009.
FRANK PRICE/A1 STEAM LOCOMOTIVE TRUST

enjoyed Mark Allatt, Chairman of the A1 Steam Locomotive Trust – *Tornado's* creator and owner – suggesting "If any of the rail operators would like to use this technology for themselves, we would be more than happy to build them an engine."

The £3 million *Tornado* had done more the day before than simply to run confidently between London and the Kent coast and back twice. On her way out from Victoria, at 5.48pm, at the head of the 'Cathedrals Express White Cliffs Christmas Dinner Special', she took a hundred stranded Kent commuters with her, dropping them off along the way in the icy dark at Swanley, Maidstone East and Canterbury West. A spokesman for Southeastern Trains congratulated Mr Allatt, who had told commuters to climb aboard, on his "moment of glory", adding "I'm sure those passengers were saved from a lengthy wait; all credit to him." And to *Tornado*.

This had been an exhilarating, and happily warm-hearted, way to round off *Tornado's* first full year on the main line. Eighteen years in the making, many people had waited a very long time indeed to see this improbable dream come true, a perfectly real recreation of a 1948 London & North Eastern Railway 'A1' Pacific 4-6-2 (a term used to explain its wheel arrangement – a four-wheel bogie, six drivers, and a trailing axle under the firebox), an express passenger steam locomotive for the 21st Century cleared to work on the nation's main lines. Perhaps the one disappointment was that Network Rail insisted that, as with preserved main line express passenger steam locomotives, *Tornado* would be restricted to a top speed of 75mph. Hopefully this will be raised to 90mph in the future. *Tornado* is perfectly capable of 100mph.

Just how many people were keen to see *Tornado* was made apparent to the railway authorities at King's Cross station on 7th February 2009, the day the apple green locomotive made her debut at the London terminus. Despite being warned by the A1 Steam Locomotive Trust that they should expect a big turnout, management were nevertheless taken by surprise when the narrow platforms of the station began to seethe with railway enthusiasts and regular passengers drawn, like moths to a glowing firebox, by the stirring sight of *Tornado* rolling her train from York imperiously down to the buffer stops. Safety, says Network Rail, the modern-day owner of the 1852 Great Northern Railway station at the foot of the East Coast Main Line, is its first consideration, and it can sometimes be believed that passengers are seen as bit of a nuisance and burden on the efficient day to day running of services from its main line and suburban platforms.

Middle managers were apoplectic when crowds not seen since the wartime evacuation of children to the provinces or perhaps VE Day began to assemble shoulder to shoulder to witness the metropolitan homecoming for an 'A1'. This was for a design of locomotive that was commonplace, indeed largely overlooked, in the years leading to its replacement by diesels from 1964.

On this unforgettable night, Network Rail realised it was powerless to react against an ocean of good-humoured faces spanning every generation. Some senior staff wanted to clear the station, but they would never have managed it, and in any case need not have feared. This was not a horde of troublemakers; this was a collection of well-wishers who simply wanted to cheer *Tornado* all the way into the station and create, to say the least, something of a stir. A few tears were shed, but not a drop of blood spilt.

The affection for *Tornado*, now a celebrity in her own steely right, was confirmed in another way. A couple of entrepreneurial A1 Trust staff grasped the opportunity to raise much-needed funds by snatching a couple of plastic buckets from the special train's mess coach. Pushing their way politely and gently through the tightly packed crowd with their containers held high, they were amazed to meet people willingly surrendering not just pennies and silver, but fivers, tenners, even £20 notes. "All I can say is just well done, well done," said one grey-haired giver.

Twelve days later, *Tornado* was back in the national news, on television, radio and the national and local press, when she was officially named by the Prince of Wales and the Duchess of Cornwall at York station. "May God bless all who are lucky enough to locomote behind her", declared Prince Charles he tugged at the embossed silk banner covering *Tornado's* newly-fitted nameplates, and a cloud of smoke from the engine's double chimney wafted across the royal presence. Undeterred, the Prince, clad in his often-seen camel coat, climbed aboard the locomotive's footplate, riding out from York under superheated steam on his way to Sheffield.

Prince Charles, an unabashed steam and railway enthusiast, has employed *Tornado* again since the naming ceremony to pull the Royal Train; in all but name, the new 'A1' is By Royal Appointment. She is also an engine with an emotional appeal that cuts right across the social spectrum and age barriers. This was made evidently clear when *Tornado* was chosen to feature on BBC 2's hugely popular, and populist, *Top Gear* motoring programme. Filmed in April 2009 and screened two months later to an audience of more than seven million people, a special edition featured a race from London to Edinburgh pitting a car against a motorbike and a railway locomotive. The car chosen was a 1949 Jaguar XK120, driven by *Top Gear* presenter James May up the 'A1' trunk road; the motorbike was a 1949 Vincent Black Shadow ridden by Richard Hammond, and the locomotive was *Tornado* fired for parts of its 393-mile run from King's Cross to Edinburgh Waverley by Jeremy Clarkson.

The outspoken and entertaining Clarkson, although pretending to despise railways, was born in Doncaster, where so many of the former LNER Pacifics had been built, including *Flying Scotsman* – the first British locomotive to officially reach 100mph – and *Mallard*, the streamlined 'A4' Pacific that, on 3rd July 1938, captured the world

HRH Prince Charles pulled the ceremonial ribbon to officially name the 50th 'A1' *Tornado* at York station on 19th February 2009. He was joined at the event by A1 Trust Chairman Mark Allatt.
NEIL WHITAKER/A1 STEAM LOCOMOTIVE TRUST

Opposite, top: *Tornado* is just the latest steam locomotive to be honoured by a member of the Royal Family. HRH the Prince of Wales sits in *Tornado's* driving seat.
ROB MORLAND/A1 STEAM LOCOMOTIVE TRUST

Opposite, below: By Royal Appointment… The Fleur de Lys is prominent attached to the front end of No. 60163 as it hurries the Royal Train towards Leeds, at Ulleskelf, on 19th February 2009.
LES NIXON

record for a steam locomotive descending Stoke Bank between Grantham and Peterborough at a maximum of 126mph. A vocal enthusiast for great British engineering, Clarkson was clearly charmed by *Tornado* despite the 75mph speed limit imposed on the locomotive. As the Pacific was up against the very fastest motorbike and sports car of 1949, it certainly had its job cut out.

On the day, *Tornado* performed well. Passengers who had booked for a journey to Scotland on board a 'Cathedrals Express' were only let into the secret – that this was to be a race filmed for *Top Gear* – at the point of departure. This was the first time in 41 years that a steam train had run all the way between King's Cross and Edinburgh. With a train of nine carmine and cream coaches weighing 375 tons (a doddle for an 'A1'), *Tornado* was expected to run to a mile-a-minute timetable. The fact that the trip was scheduled to take just over eight hours was not because *Tornado* was unable to run faster, but because of the need to stop four times – at Grantham, York, Newcastle and Berwick – for water. Non-stop steam trains between King's Cross and Edinburgh, beginning with the 'Capitals United' in 1949, had been possible because of the many water-troughs laid out along the main line; locomotives were able to scoop thousands of gallons of water into their tenders while running at full speed, a luxury *Tornado* and her crew had to do without 60 years on. If the troughs had survived, and worked, the train would easily have won the *Top Gear* race.

In the event, the times taken by *Tornado* to reach Peterborough, Grantham and York were all preservation era records. The steam train arrived just ahead of time at Waverley in exactly eight hours. Clarkson rushed from the footplate to the official finishing line at

Tornado was given a rapturous reception when it reached Edinburgh Waverley station on 28th February 2009. The 'Auld Reekie Express' was its first excursion into Scotland.
EDDIE BOBROWSKI

A blackened *Top Gear* presenter Jeremy Clarkson had his work cut out firing *Tornado* on the race from London to Scotland. But for water stops, the 'A1' might have won the race against a 1949 Jaguar XK120 car and a 1949 Vincent Black Shadow motorcycle.
DANNY HOPKINS/STEAM RAILWAY

the bar of the Balmoral Hotel, but only to find James May already there; he had beaten the train, he said, by 'no more than ten minutes'. The Vincent Black Shadow, meanwhile, had broken down a long way south of the Scottish border.

As a funny ending, Clarkson, sweaty, black-faced and utterly filthy in his dark blue boiler suit, was invited to pose with a wedding party in the hotel; the bride had mistaken him for a traditional lucky chimney sweep. This was a delightful end to a brilliant bit of television. *Tornado* was as much, and perhaps even more, the star of the show than the naturally domineering Clarkson. She had certainly won many new fans.

And, yet, *Tornado* was also proving popular with professional engineers. Even though the steam age on the railways was essentially a thing of the past, it was hard for even the most forward-looking engineer not to have a soft spot for this compelling machine and especially so for those who, against the grain and all the odds, had designed and built her, and put her into such convincing service on the 21st Century main line. In the month following the *Top Gear* race, the A1 Trust received two highly-regarded accolades. These were the Sir Henry Royce Foundation Memorial Award for excellence in engineering and the IMechE [Institute of Mechanical Engineers] Engineering Heritage Award.

Throughout 2010, *Tornado* continued to delight enthusiasts and the public alike.

Whenever and wherever she appeared – always looking just a little haughty – the tracks she rode became the railway's equivalent of the catwalks of the fashion world. *Tornado* had become an unlikely mechanical supermodel as well as a national celebrity. There are many other steam locomotives, equally impressive, running special trains on very many days of the year across the length and breadth of Britain.

So, what makes *Tornado* stand out? Why does she draw the crowds, feature on popular television and radio shows as well as taking generous space in national and local newspapers? The answer is not simply that she is a particularly fine example of an express passenger steam locomotive, but that she is brand new. This in itself is not a virtue, yet *Tornado's* very existence is a kind of modern miracle and one, perhaps, that could only happen in Britain. Why? Not so very deep down, many people in an ostensibly super-modern, digital age, have a hankering for beautiful machinery, for things well crafted and honestly made; for machines made not far away by cheap, and even child, labour in distant lands, but by ordinary decent people in the very towns that, famous for their engineering and productive prowess until recent decades, have lost what had once seemed their right to craft magnificent machines that everyone involved in their making could rightly be proud of.

Tornado is a reminder of a Britain before the overwhelming triumph of consumer culture, proof that we can make machines that not only do a fine job, and are inherently rewarding to make, but also have the ability to move us to our very core. Of course, *Tornado* can move us over long distances, too, and in all weathers. Whether or not *Tornado* was to have remained a one-off, though, was something that had been running through the minds of the members of the A1 Steam Locomotive Trust for most of the 18 years it took to build the 50th 'A1' (the earlier 49 had all been constructed, at Doncaster and Darlington, in less than 18 months).

In June 2010, the Trust announced that it had started a feasibility study into building a second main line steam locomotive, a London & North Eastern Railway [LNER] Gresley 'P2' 2-8-2. The first of these superb-looking and charismatic machines, No. 2001 *Cock o' The North*, designed to haul the heaviest express trains over the hilly route north of Edinburgh, took to the rails in 1934. Only a handful of people remain who can remember how it looked and sounded, and the Trust believes that they are well-equipped to rectify a small number of design defects that contributed to its early demise. Rebuilt into a cumbersome 'Pacific' by Gresley's intolerant successor Edward Thompson, it slipped into the scrapyard in 1959 almost unnoticed.

As Mark Allatt said at the time, "The 'P2' is the most requested locomotive the Trust is asked to build next. In addition to its striking looks, incredible power and undoubted glamour it also has around 70 per cent commonality with *Tornado* , including the boiler, tender and many other detailed fittings." Only six of these mighty locomotives were built. No. 2007, and whatever suitably Scottish name would grace it, would make a fine running partner for *Tornado*.

The success of *Tornado* has encouraged attempts both in Britain and around the world to build new steam locomotives. The majority of these are plans for long-vanished types. Every steam enthusiast will have a mental list of engines he or she would like to see running again; there are, however, plans afoot, too, for a new generation of high speed (125mph upwards) and super-efficient steam locomotives, notably the '5AT' 4-6-0 designed by the contemporary steam engineer David Wardale, currently based in Inverness. This is a fairly small locomotive – about the same size as a Stanier 'Black Five' mixed traffic 4-6-0 – but one that, if built, would pack a tremendous punch. Where a 'Black Five', fine machine though it is, would be hard-pressed to produce much more than 1,800ihp [indicated horsepower; the power generated in the cylinders and the best measure of the all out power of a steam locomotive] and has run at up to 96mph, a '5AT' would be able to generate 3,500ihp more or less continuously while, also, being able to maintain its 125mph top speed over long distances. Although much detailed work has been done, the '5AT' project still lacks the finance that might yet see it streaking along the country's main lines as fast as contemporary diesel and electric expresses.

Can this scene be recreated again in a few years time – a classic original Gresley 4-6-2 with the designer's powerful masterpiece, the 2-8-2 'P2'? 'A1' No. 4479 *Robert the Devil* leaves King's Cross to set off northwards with an express on 1st June 1934 as pioneer semi-streamlined 'P2' No. 2001 *Cock o'The North* waits alongside.
F. R. HEBRON/RAIL ARCHIVE STEPHENSON

Wardale's mentor, the great Argentine steam engineer Livio Dante Porta [1922-2003] contacted the A1 Trust as soon as he learned about the plan to build a new 'A1' suggesting that the design might be brought up to date. This, though, was never really the idea behind *Tornado*. The locomotive that brings so much delight to so many people on British main lines today is very much a replacement for a class of highly-regarded British express steam locomotives that, finally taken out of service in 1966, were all scrapped even though members of the class awaiting the cutter's gas axe could have been bought at the time for the price of a new E-Type Jaguar.

It just wasn't easy to purchase a steam locomotive at the time. Even if you had the money, there was BR bureaucracy to deal with. BR was on a 'modernisation or die' kick, and insistent that any purchase had to be removed from the railway it used to operate on. What point, therefore, was there in placing a 100mph engine in a backyard, any more that it made sense to try and buy the Cunard liner *Queen Elizabeth* and moor it in a boating lake. Holiday camp entrepreneur Billy Butlin did buck the trend, and his lasting memorials include London Midland & Scottish [LMS] star performing 4-6-0 No. 6100 *Royal Scot* and two heavyweight 'Duchess Coronation' 4-6-2s, one of which is now in the National Collection at York and recently restreamlined. It is a sad story however that his agent's attempt to purchase the pioneer East Coast 'A4' No. 60014 *Silver Link* failed on cost grounds, and after Doncaster Council also apathetically turned its back, the famous streamliner went to the torch at its Doncaster Works birthplace in the autumn of 1963.

Despite looking like something from the 1940s, *Tornado* incorporates a great deal of new technology to keep it up to the minute in terms of demands placed on it by the operating authorities. While it would be good, one day in the not so distant future, to see a brand new type of steam locomotive on the rails, *Tornado* represents a tradition of British engine building that can be traced directly back to George and Robert Stephenson and the *Rocket*. The 'A1s' had rivals in their heyday, from 1948 to 1966, yet *Tornado* exists to evoke the best of British steam locomotive engineering of 60 years ago. Every time she steams out of a terminus or races along the nation's main lines, photographers and amateur filmmakers in tow, our collective heart beats that little bit faster. A three-cylinder beat that is: jazzy, racy and as thrilling as it was in 1948 when the very first 'A1', No. 60114 *W. P. Allen* emerged from Doncaster Works for the Eastern Region of British Railways, just three months before the Prince of Wales emerged at Buckingham Palace...

CHAPTER TWO

Peppercorn's 'A1s'
More hunters
than racehorses

W. *P. Allen* was not exactly an inspiring name for the first of a brand new class of express passenger steam locomotives. This though was the prosaic legend attached to the smoke deflectors of the very first of the new generation 'A1' Pacifics a few weeks after she emerged from Doncaster Works in August 1948, carrying the nationalised five-digit number 60114 instead of the LNER's intended No. 114.

Earlier LNER Pacifics, the elite of the express passenger fleet, had revelled in names like *Flying Scotsman*, *Silver Link*, *Hyperion* and *Prince Palatine*. Equally, though, records show that the naming of express locomotives had long been a hit and miss affair; a streamlined LNER 'A4' Pacific named *Gannet* sounded anything but glamorous. Earlier Gresley 'A3' Pacifics had been named after famous racehorses. Some of these seem decidedly banal, and even downright funny today: *Sandwich*, *Pretty Polly*, *Robert the Devil*, *Call Boy*, *Brown Jack*, and *Gay Crusader*.

Because, though, the 'A1' Pacifics emerged just months after the LNER had been incorporated into the state-owned British Railways, a creation of Clement Attlee's radical and reforming Labour government that had ousted Winston Churchill in the 1945 General Election, it had seemed a soundly socialist idea to name the first of the new engines – the last of a line of LNER Pacifics dating from 1922 – after a trade unionist. So *W. P. Allen* it had it to be. Bill Allen was a prominent trade union official, the General Secretary of ASLEF [Association of Locomotive Engineers and Firemen] who had begun his career as a cleaner on the old Great Northern Railway, rising to become a member of the new post-war Railway Executive.

The 'A1s' had emerged from a programme, created in 1945, aiming to build 16 new 6ft 8in Pacifics along the lines of the rebuilt No. 4470 *Great Northern* [later classified 'A1/1' and numbered No. 60113]. This was Thompson's reconstruction of Gresley's very first Pacific, a swan transformed into an ugly duckling, that had emerged from Doncaster Works, to the horror of Gresley enthusiasts inside and outside the LNER, in September 1945. Thompson won permission to build a further 33 express passenger Pacifics in 1946, all of them intended to be robust, post-war machines well able to deal with an era of heavy trains, reduced maintenance, patchy coal supplies and a shortage of labour. The LNER was certainly in a hurry to build them, and not least, perhaps, because the nationalisation of the railways was on the cards and the chance to build specifically LNER locomotives might well be coming to an end. In the event, all 49 of the Pacifics Thompson won permission to build were Peppercorn engines: the 'A1s'.

W. P. Allen, doyen of the class, proved to be a fast, powerful and reliable locomotive as were all the new 'A1s'. She was withdrawn from service on Boxing Day 1964 and scrapped the following year at Blyth, Northumberland. Curiously none of the following 'A1s' were named until 18 months after *W. P. Allen* first turned a wheel. This was possibly because the new state Railway Executive was keen not to be seen wasting public money on such frivolity. When they did come, though, the names were often inspired. They resulted from an initiative driven by the Railway Correspondence & Travel Society, which knew it was pushing at an open door because some of its senior members also happened to hold high office in the nationalised railway and were therefore closet enthusiasts. The second of the batch was dubbed *Meg Merrilies*, which sounds fast, as the 'A1s' were. The third was *Hal o' The Wynd*. This sounds quick, too; faster than fairies, faster than witches. *Peregrine*, *Kestrel*, *King's Courier*, *Alcazar* and *Foxhunter* all suited engines capable of topping 100mph. *Archibald Sturrock*, *Patrick Stirling* and *Edward Fletcher* might have seemed a little dull, yet these were the names of some of the great locomotive engineers of the past.

Great Central and *Great Eastern* commemorated much-loved railways that had been swallowed up in the 'grouping' of 1923, a process of rationalisation that had seen Britain's many and varied railways compressed into a 'Big Four', one of which was the LNER, the first in Britain to run a fleet of high-speed Pacific locomotives and the first to plunge headlong into streamlining and speeds of 100mph on a more or less everyday basis by

Turned out in pristine condition by its home shed of Heaton (Newcastle), No. 60116 *Hal O' The Wynd* backs out of King's Cross after bringing in a train from its home city in July 1962. The engine is in its final paint style of Brunswick green.
GEOFF RIXON

the late 1930s. Only *Auld Reekie* seemed a bit hard on a fast engine that was anything but old and not even particulary 'reekie' by the standards of steam locomotives. The name, of course, was an old one long given to the city of Edinburgh, a haunt of all 49 'A1s' and their direct descendant, *Tornado*, today.

The 'A1s' were built at Doncaster and Darlington works during 1948 and 1949. They had been designed under the gentle and subtle direction of Arthur Peppercorn, the last Chief Mechanical Engineer [CME] of the LNER. 'Pepp', as he was fondly known, was one of the best-loved of all British steam locomotive engineers. He took up office late in his, and the LNER's, day on 1st June 1946, and yet in the three years left to him on the railways, he oversaw the design and development of the 'A1' and 'A2' Pacifics, the former with long-legged 6ft 8in driving wheels, the latter with 6ft 2in drivers better for tackling Scottish hills. Both classes gave back to the LNER, and to the Eastern, North Eastern and Scottish Regions of British Railways, an elegance of line that had been nurtured by Sir Nigel Gresley (Chief Mechanical Engineer of the Great Northern and LNER from 1911 until his death on 5 April 1941) until this was wilfully undermined by his tight-lipped successor, Edward Thompson, CME from 1941 until his retirement five years later.

Where Thompson had believed in efficiency, reliability and serviceability at all costs, Peppercorn appreciated elegance as much as these necessary qualities, just as Gresley had done before him. And, so although Peppercorn's Pacifics were born into a post-war world that demanded low-cost maintenance and, by extension, rugged simplicity, they were nevertheless visually well-balanced, even handsome machines, evoking power, speed and durability.

Arthur Peppercorn, like so many distinguished British locomotive engineers, was the son of a clergyman; steam and the Church of England seemed to have gone together prayer book-in-cylinder. Born, one of eleven children, on 29th January 1889 in Stoke Prior near Leominster, Herefordshire (the church had been entirely rebuilt in 1863), Pepp upset his father early in life by declaring he wanted to be an engine driver. The Rev Alfred Thomas Peppercorn sent his son to Hereford Cathedral School hoping, in vein, to change the boy's mind. In 1905 Pepp was taken on as a premium apprentice at the Great Northern Railway works at Doncaster. One of his fellow apprentices, and a lifelong friend, was W. O. Bentley, who left the railways to set up his famous, Le Mans-winning car business immediately after the First World War. Ettore Bugatti, Bentley's greatest rival on the racing circuit, described W. O.'s rugged cars as the 'world's fastest lorries.' But, these great green cars, with their Gothic radiators, were more express railway locomotives built for the roads than 'lorries' for the race track; W. O. had been trained at Doncaster, and something of the Great Northern and its fine tradition of elegant and robust engineering stayed with him.

Peppercorn also struck up a friendship with Herbert Nigel Gresley (another son of a clergyman) who was soon to become the Chief Mechanical Engineer of the Great Northern, and, without doubt, one of Britain's greatest locomotive engineers. A gentlemanly

Arthur Henry Peppercorn (born 29th January 1889) was rarely photographed outside official circles. His early death on 3rd March 1951 robbed steam of one of its finest chief engineers and designers.

THE SCIENCE & SOCIETY PICTURE LIBRARY

sportsman, Peppercorn, who had been a keen rugby and cricket player in his time, would travel up by train to Scotland with Gresley in later years to indulge their common pastime, fishing. The easy-going Peppercorn was a happy foil to the dynamic and ambitious Gresley; and yet Gresley could spot a deceptively intelligent and highly organised mind behind Pepp's bluff and jovial façade.

A Royal Engineer serving in France as technical assistant to the CME of the Directorate of Transportation during the First World War, Peppercorn returned to the GNR and, over the next 20 years, more or less shadowed Edward Thompson, acting as the autocratic, Cambridge-educated Thompson's assistant on three occasions.

The two men became awkwardly close from 1941 when Thompson, now CME at Doncaster would telephone Pepp in the evenings asking him to come over to discuss some design detail or other. Having recently lost his wife, Thompson, a shy and difficult man, was lonely. Peppercorn, by contrast, was a genial fellow who liked nothing better than to put work behind him at the end of a long day. In any case, widowed himself, he had recently begun stepping out with a delightful and good-looking young woman; they were married in 1948. Dorothy Mather, as she later became, was a natural choice to become Honorary President of the A1 Steam Locomotive Trust, and was there to launch *Tornado* when she turned a wheel under steam for the first time in August 2008. Dorothy (known as Pat, then), was very much a railway wife.

"I used to take the ladies, doctors' wives and so forth, for trips around the works", she says. "It was rather noisy, but the railways were part and parcel of our lives." Pat was unsure about Thompson. "I was with the Coal Commission during the War. I met Pepp there. He was thirty years older than me. A lovely man, kind and very funny. He was working under Thompson. Do you know what Thompson said? If Pepp married me, he would never get the CME's job. Well..."

Thompson may have been jealous, yet Pepp did get the job. Most awkward of all, though, for Peppercorn was the fact that Thompson had been on a crusade to redesign Gresley's legendary Pacifics. He thought them too complicated, and went so far as to rebuild his predecessor's very first Pacific, No. 4470 *Great Northern*, first built in 1922, into one of the ugliest of all British express passenger locomotives. J. F. 'Freddie' Harrison, one of Gresley's assistants, recalled later that LNER board members "tried hard to persuade Thompson to take any of the Pacifics except the first; but he would have none of it." Thompson was, in fact, planning to rid the LNER of all Gresley Pacifics and, indeed, most of Gresley's locomotives. Might a part of the reason be that Thompson was the son-in-law of Sir Vincent Raven (another clergyman's son), the last CME of the North Eastern Railway, and was loyal to what he might have seen as a wronged memory? After all, it was Gresley who had promoted his own design for the GNR 'A1' Pacifics over Raven's rival NER 'A2' Pacifics after the formation of the LNER. One of these, No. 2402 *City of York*, was the first locomotive built for the LNER to be scrapped. The original five 'A2s' had all gone by May 1937. Had Thompson seen this as a slight on his family?

Thompson (the son of a headmaster) would never have admitted to such an emotional response even if it had contained a grain of truth. In public, he was always the rationalist, with plans, when he took over from Gresley, for ten new standard types of steam locomotives for the LNER covering all traffic requirements. Much has been said about Thompson that is unkind. In his defence, P. J. Coster, writing in the Journal of the Stephenson Locomotive Society, says he "was appointed at a time when Gresley's locomotives were not to be seen in the kindliest of lights, their many weaknesses exposed by the lack of skilled maintenance upon which the high quality of their performance depended almost entirely. Thompson had endured years of subordination to the brilliant and unorthodox leadership at Doncaster... and no doubt suffered the arrival of the latest marvel from Doncaster with a suspicious eye... Thompson had a considerable task in following a man such as Gresley, and the size of his professional task in halting the avalanche of failures, restoring some sense of order and something of reliability to the motive power department out of overwhelming chaos would have brought many men close to despair."

The jury, considering the perceived weaknesses of Gresley's Pacifics, especially at the time Thompson took over the reins at Doncaster, is still out. While it was true that Gresley's very particular conjugated valve gear gave trouble during those dark days of the Second World War, the very same engines went on to perform brilliantly in BR days and right up to their last great success, the running of the accelerated three-hour Aberdeen to Glasgow expresses in the 1960s. Had there really been anything wrong with Gresley's designs? As Malcolm Crawley, Chairman of the Gresley Society, points out, "Sir Nigel continued with the conjugated valve gear because it worked and worked well. It became a problem only in wartime because of reduced ability to do maintenance, and because staff failed to close the access door, thus allowing the ingress of ash, a wonderful grinding paste when mixed with the grease in the bearings. Thompson intended to rebuild many of the Gresley locomotives. He didn't do so, largely because his rebuilds were often not as good as the originals."

Thompson's own prototype 'A1' Pacific certainly lacked the grace, and perhaps deliberately so, of Gresley's beautiful mechanical racehorses. In Doncaster drawing office, however, and unbeknown to the unpopular Thompson, draftsmen with a huge respect for Gresley were busy shaping designs for altogether better-looking engines for the future. When Thompson strode past the long line of their desks, these draftsmen, it is said, hid their latest drawings from him. They showed them willingly to Peppercorn who, of course, loyal to the memory and engineering of Gresley, kept knowingly quiet.

When Thompson retired, Peppercorn immediately surrounded himself with assistants who, although forward-looking, were loyal to the spirit of Gresley and to his high aesthetic as well as engineering standards. Peppercorn brought Freddie Harrison, an engineer intimately associated with the future generation of 'A1s', down from Scotland to be his deputy. He also brought back Gresley's former technical assistant Bert Spencer along with Teddy Windle as Chief Draughtsman, among others exiled to outposts of the LNER during the hard-nosed Thompson years.

Unsurprisingly, Peppercorn created an exceptionally good-natured and happy office. He allowed his assistants to get on with their jobs as they best saw fit. His dry humour, perfect manners and straightforward kindness endeared him to everyone who worked for him. He never swore, or treated subordinates with anything other than courtesy. Resistant to honours, Pepp's reign [CMEs were very much the kings of their industrial realms] came to an end all too briefly. At his retirement dinner, he was presented with a perfect scale model, built by Doncaster apprentices, of his very first Pacific, the 'A2' numbered No. 525 and named *A. H. Peppercorn* (the original plan to name it *Arthur Peppercorn* was abandoned because nameplates with his name spelt out were too long to fit on the smoke deflectors). Typically, Pepp was moved to tears. In later years, Dorothy Mather found the model too big for her new home in North Yorkshire; she gave it to Colonel Hugh Rogers, a friend and author of *Thompson and Peppercorn: Locomotive Engineers.*

What Peppercorn and team needed to do was to develop the LNER Pacifics into machines better able to stand up to the rough and tumble conditions on the post-war railways. That they should be elegant machines no-one on Peppercorn's team doubted, and yet they had to be more reliable, easier to maintain and able to withstand less loving treatment than Gresley's thoroughbreds had in the 1920s and 1930s. Just as 'fitness for purpose' and 'functionalism' had become the buzzwords in contemporary industrial design and architecture, so these applied to the design of post-war steam locomotives, too. In any case, the 'A1s' were not to be built as the 'A4s' had been for pure speed. No, their role as far as the design team was concerned was to haul 600-ton expresses, without fireworks but with immense economy and efficiency.

Peppercorn even travelled to North America as part of a deputation of LNER and LMS officials to study the latest technical scene and to see how US and Canadian practice could be transferred usefully to the post-war British railway scene. As E. S. 'Stuart' Cox, an LMS engineer who later chaired the BR Standard locomotive design committee, recalled, "the party of six set sail on the *Queen Elizabeth* in October 1945 in company with 11,000 Canadian soldiers returning home on a ship still in wartime guise. The normally luxurious cabins had been gutted, and each now held eight makeshift bunks in two-tier pairs. Only two meals a day were served, and the ship was dry. Groups of hard bitten officers in the lounge looked distinctly thoughtful over their nightly intake of Coca Cola!" Landing at Halifax, the team went on to New York and spent 52 days visiting nine major railroads and the major rolling stock builders. Peppercorn, Cox and Co covered 5,000 miles by New World trains. They rode on, and behind, such magnificent new locomotives as Paul Kiefer's New York Central 'Niagara' class 4-8-4s and watched the most powerful of all steam locomotives, the Chesapeake & Ohio 'T8' 2-6-6-6 'Mallets' in action in and around Richmond, Virginia.

Well aware of the – admittedly imperfect – diesel revolution in evidence all around them, the British team were, nevertheless, fascinated by the way their American counterparts had grown steam locomotives to such a great size and were able to run them over vast mileages with a considerable degree of overall efficiency and reliability. Although there had been plans, at LNER board level, to buy pairs of 1,600hp diesel-electrics to replace the railway's fleet of steam Pacifics, this never happened. Under Cox, and his British Transport Executive boss, R. A. 'Robin' Riddles, steam was to hold sway in Britain for another generation. Freddie Harrison, the lead designer on the 'A1' team, was a Yorkshireman who had intended to join the army but, diverted by the sight and sound of steam, joined the Great Northern at Doncaster as a premium apprentice under Gresley in 1921. Harrison, who went on to become Chief Mechanical Engineer [CME] of British Railways, in 1958, lived long enough to give valuable advice to the A1 Steam Locomotive Trust. He had been tipped widely to succeed Gresley as the LNER's CME, but was too young at the time of the former's death; and so the job passed to Thompson.

Harrison had known Thompson well. He told the railway historian Colonel H. C. B. Rogers, "E. T. was in many ways an extraordinary, unpredictable character who, when he wished, could charm a bird off the proverbial tree, and yet, at other times, could be ruthless – nearly sadistic! All the time, he had at the back of his mind a determination to undermine Gresley's reputation." Harrison suggested that despite his outward rationalism, Thompson was full of ideas, many of them impractical; when these were rejected, as apparently they often were, by Gresley, Thompson felt insulted; and, he was a man who harboured grievances. Thompson was also something of a dandy. Harrison said he had over 50 tailor-made suits, around a hundred shirts and many pairs of immaculately polished shoes. Photographs do indeed reveal an impeccably dressed gentleman, and yet he was clearly unable to translate his fine sense of couture to the design of express passenger steam locomotives.

Peppercorn's team, working in a far friendlier atmosphere than had been the case under Thompson, did well, in a very short time, to produce machines that were fundamentally reliable, efficient, fast, powerful and reasonably economical to run. That they continued the line of Gresley's Pacifics in terms of style and essential character was a bonus.

Peppercorn's 'A1s' and 'A2s' were, perhaps, more hunters than racehorses, but after the hiatus of the Thompson regime, when aesthetics were hurled unceremoniously from locomotive chimneys, it was good to see a fleet of modern engines that truly belonged to an artistic design tradition that stretched back to the much-loved and extremely beautiful 'Eight Foot Singles' of Patrick Stirling, Chief Mechanical Engineer of the Great Northern Railway from 1866–95, dying in office at the age of 75. These 4-2-2 locomotives ran like sewing machines and had well and truly captured the imagination of the public and railway folk alike.

By the 1920s, however, far more powerful locomotives had been needed. Nigel Gresley's genius had been to invest in big, powerful locomotives – and lots of them – that would

Overleaf: The last of the original 'A1s' to be completed was also one of the shortest-lived. A Scottish example, No. 60162, and not yet named *Saint Johnstoun*, rumbles through Kinross Junction. The original 'stovepipe' chimney fitted to the engines can be seen to good effect.
W. J. VERDEN ANDERSON/RAIL ARCHIVE STEPHENSON

manage pretty much anything thrown at them by the LNER's operating departments in the foreseeable future. When his first Pacific, No. 4470 *Great Northern*, appeared at King's Cross on 7th April 1922 for its official inspection and display to the general public, it caused quite a sensation. *Great Northern* was a giant by contemporary British standards. She was also very good-looking indeed: long, lithe and suggestive of mercurial speed and prodigious power.

Gresley had, in fact, proposed a Pacific as early as 1915. This four-cylinder machine, however, was little more than a stretched version of H. A. Ivatt's sturdy and successful large-boilered Great Northern 'C1' Atlantic [4-4-2] of 1902. Between outline proposals for the Ivatt-style Pacific and the debut of *Great Northern*, Gresley had studied the latest developments in locomotive design in the United States. The design that most affected him was that of the Pennsylvania Railroad's 'K4' Pacific developed jointly with Alco [the American Locomotive Company]. These were modified over several decades and were one of the outstanding American steam locomotives.

And, yet, Gresley still had lessons to learn. When, in 1925, his 'A1' Pacifics Nos. 4474 *Victor Wild* and 2545 *Diamond Jubilee* were put on test on the main lines from King's Cross and Paddington against the Great Western Railway's far smaller 'Castle' Class 4-6-0s, Nos. 4073 *Caerphilly Castle* and 4074 *Caldicot Castle*, the LNER engines were soundly beaten. Yes, the 'A1s' could pull hard and run fast, but at the expense of voracious coal and water consumption; by contrast, the 'Castles', designed at Swindon under its CME Charles Collett, nibbled coal and sipped water. This was all to do with the efficient way the Great Western engines used the steam produced in their high-pressure boilers; this passed freely to pistons and cylinders whereas the 'A1s', old-fashioned in this respect, were slightly choked as they ran fast and hard. Gresley learned lessons from Swindon and quickly began work upgrading the 'A1' to a new 'Super Pacific', the 'A3'. Appearing from 1928, these were truly fine express engines, owing something to American and something to Swindon practice, the latter having been much influenced by the latest developments in France, the leading country in terms of the efficient use of steam up until the last main-line locomotives were built there in the late 1940s.

The economical 'A3s' proved they could run the 268 miles from King's Cross to Newcastle in under four hours and sprint up to 108mph. Gresley followed up with the legendary streamlined 'A4' Pacifics of 1935. These has been commissioned specifically to run the LNER's revolutionary 'Silver Jubilee' express introduced that year between King's Cross and Newcastle and back running at an average speed of 70.4mph. This was some going at the time when few British expresses were timed at much above an average of 60mph. The challenge had come from a number of sources: inter-city air services, faster roads and, just as importantly, international rivalry. In 1933, the Deutsche Reichsbahn had accelerated its new streamlined, two-car diesel train, 'Fliegende Hamburger' [the 'Flying Hamburger'] to run from Berlin to Hamburg, a distance of 178.1 miles in just 138 minutes; this spelt an average speed of 77.4mph and speeds of 100mph on every trip.

Gresley asked the German Railways and the builders of their high-speed diesels how quickly they could run a similar train comprising three cars from King's Cross to Newcastle. The reply was four-and-a-quarter hours. Gresley believed, quite rightly, that he could do better with steam and much heavier trains, complete with a full hot meal service rather than the 'Fliegende Hamburger's' cold snack menu. In the event – and what a remarkable event it was – Gresley and his team designed and built the first 'A4' Pacific, No. 2509 *Silver Link*, and the new seven-coach streamlined train in just 25 weeks. If this was astonishing by the far tardier standards of 2010, so was the performance. Straight from Doncaster Works and with virtually no time for testing or running in, the 'A4' headed a press demonstration run of the 'Silver Jubilee' out of King's Cross on 27th September 1935.

Here was a train, the TGV or Eurostar of its day, that thrilled everyone – an enormous crowd – who saw it leave King's Cross at 2.25pm and plunge, like some silver wraith, into Gasworks and Copenhagen tunnels north of the London terminus as it began the long climb up to Hitchin before gaining the LNER's racing ground across the Fens through Bedfordshire and Huntingdonshire. Climbing in the 90s, *Silver Link* crossed the 100mph threshold at milepost 30; from there the speed was above 100mph for the next twenty-five miles, reaching a maximum of 112.5mph twice. By the time the train drew into Peterborough, it had averaged 100mph for 43 miles on end. The 'Flying Hamburger' seemed little more than a cheap sausage. Quite what Driver Arthur Taylor, Fireman Luty and Locomotive Running Superintendent I. S. W. Groom up on the footplate must have thought we can only guess: no British steam crew had run anything remotely like as fast as this before.

The ride had certainly been a bit choppy at times, as Cecil J. Allen, the railway historian who rode and timed the record-breaker, recalled. While climbing up to St Neots at 104.5mph, "by now there had drifted into my compartment Sir Nigel himself [he was, in fact, knighted the following year by Edward VIII], completely imperturbable, armed with a chronograph watch of vast dimensions which he had had made specially for speed recording purposes. He sat down next to me, and beyond him Chas J. Brown, Chief Civil Engineer... the latter was a nervous man, and his face betrayed the fact by being some shades paler than normally. On the opposite seat sat Randolph Churchill, collecting impressions of the run for the *Daily Mail*, and in search of some facts about the speed. With every fresh lurch of our coach, the Chief Mechanical Engineer directed shafts of wit at the Chief Civil Engineer concerning the condition of the latter's track, not altogether appreciated by the recipient!"

In July 1937, the LNER followed up with the 'Coronation', a garter blue streamline train running from King's Cross to Edinburgh Waverley in just six hours, with a very fast timing to York at an average speed of 71.9mph. The new nine-car train was half as heavy again as the 'Silver Jubilee'. Like its predecessor, it was a triumph, hugely popular, profitable, extremely reliable and as glamorous as any rival form of transport by air, land or sea. The first of the 'A4s' to be equipped with scientifically-improved exhausts and chimneys, derived from the researches of Andre Chapelon, the greatest of all steam locomotive engineers, in France and the Finnish driver-engineer, Kylala, emerged from Doncaster in spring 1938. This was No. 4468 *Mallard*. On 3rd July, she flew down five miles of Stoke Bank at an average speed of 120.4mph peaking, for a short distance, at 126mph. A world record that has never been beaten.

If Gresley had supplied the LNER with supremely fast and increasingly efficient Pacifics, he had also created a large number of very strong machines. During the Second World War, 'A4s' pulled trains of up to 25 carriages, weighing up to 850 tons fully loaded with troops and hemmed-in civilians, up and down the East Coast Main Line at highly creditable speeds. There was, though, a problem: Gresley's express locomotives had an Achilles' heel; this was his 'conjugated motion' that, transferring power from pistons and cylinders to each of his Pacific's six 6ft 8inch driving wheels, tended to run hot and fail if maintenance slipped, as it often did during the war years.

This was why, in part, Edward Thompson, was so zealously keen to rebuild Gresley's Pacifics, his 'P2' 2-8-2s and pretty much any other of his machines he could get his hands on. The war had highlighted the weak points of Gresley's thoroughbreds and, in any case, there would, in the foreseeable future, be little or no time, and much less money, to spend on such apparently filigree or over-sensitive design. What was needed, above all, was clarity and straightforward, no-frills design.

Even Thompson continued to design three-cylinder Pacifics when the best North American practice suggested that two-cylinders could do the job perfectly well. Actually, this wasn't quite fair, as railroads across the Atlantic enjoyed the advantage of an extremely generous loading gauge (the measure of just how big a locomotive or train can be on any given line). Britain's railways were altogether smaller than their American counterparts; if a locomotive was to have the same or more power than a three-cylinder 'A3' or 'A4' with just two cylinders, then those cylinders would have to be very big. In practice, these would foul platforms and prove a nuisance elsewhere. So, British engineers tended to opt for three or four smaller cylinders when more power was needed; multi-cylindered engines – just as in cars or motorcycles – also give a smoother ride, delivering their power in rapier rather than broadsword fashion.

The difference in sound these cylinder arrangements make is both fascinating and delightful. Where two cylinder engines thump away solidly, four-cylinder engines roar purposefully, and three-cylinder locomotives, like *Tornado*, chatter excitedly at speed. Unless you are wholly tone deaf, you could never mistake a two-cylinder British Railways' Standard Britannia-class Pacific for a four-cylinder LMS 'Duchess Coronation' Pacific, much less a three-cylinder LNER machine like *Flying Scotsman*, *Mallard*, *A. H. Peppercorn* or *Tornado*.

Peppercorn's 'A1s were essentially simple machines. They adopted everything that was best in Gresley's designs, but were easier to maintain. Their basic architecture and

Overleaf: Gresley's magnificent 'P2', *Cock 'o The North*. Wartime conditions prevented many of its minor design imperfections being resolved, but there was no questioning its stunning appearance. It's easy to see how these powerful locomotive created a stir in 1930s Britain.
RAIL ARCHIVE STEPHENSON

specification was very much in line with precedent set in the late 1930s. Indeed, as J. F. Harrison was to say in his presidential address to the Institution of Locomotive Engineers in 1961, the Peppercorn 'A1' was the kind of locomotive Gresley would have designed had he still been alive at the time. This, of course, was conjecture on Harrison's part; his revered former chief had, in fact, been working up a design for a very powerful three-cylinder express passenger 4-8-2 complete with his controversial conjugated motion in the immediate lead up to the Second World War. There were even outline drawings of a 4-8-4, both plain and streamlined. Gresley, a big man in every way, was a Big Engine man. Would Pepp's 'A1' have been enough for him in the late 1940s?

Still, Peppercorn did his best to enlarge the basic Gresley Pacific within the confines of the British loading gauge and the meagre budget available to him. Compared with the pre-war 'A4s', the new 'A1s' featured much larger grates – at 50 sq ft, the size of a small room, and all the better to burn lower qualities of coal in – larger diameter piston-valves (10 inches rather than nine inches, for easy steaming, free running and low fuel consumption), but otherwise their boilers, although a little shorter, were much the same, both with a maximum diameter of 6ft 5inches and pressed to 250 lb/sq in. *W. P. Allen's* driving wheels were the same diameter as those of *Mallard* and the Gresley and Peppercorn locomotives were of a similar mass, the 'A1s' weighing, with their eight-wheeled tenders, 164.5 tons.

Peter Townend, shedmaster at King's Cross in the late 1950s and early 1960s, says that the 'A1s' were meant to be, and were, more powerful than the Gresley 'A4s'. The bigger grate, though, was designed because "it was anticipated after the nationalisation of the coal industry [this had been on the cards during the war years as had the nationalisation of the railways themselves], you would no longer be able to buy your coal from the desired colliery." Until the Second World War, many British express passengers locomotives had been fed only the very best coal from select mines. The design of specific grates for specific locomotives was even determined to a marked extent by the nature and calorific value of coal from specific collieries. Increasingly, locomotives running in the post-war years had to take their luck as far as coal supplies went. As there was no

Now in his 80s, former King's Cross shedmaster Peter Townend, pictured at his home in Paignton in 1995, has been a valuable source of knowledge for the A1 Steam Locomotive Trust. He was responsible for getting them into daily service on the East Coast Main Line towards the end of their careers.
TED PARKER/A1 STEAM LOCOMOTIVE TRUST

guarantee of quality, it made sense for designers to allow for large grates that would burn sufficient qualities of varying qualities of coal to raise sufficient steam.

"In practice, though", continues Townend, "the higher potential power [of the 'A1s'] was not required later in the 1950s as the demands were within the capacity of the 'A4' particularly after the Kylchap blastpipes were fitted, as were the 'A1s' from new."

Where the Peppercorn engines differed markedly from the Gresley Pacifics, streamline casing aside, was in the their use of three conventional, and thoroughly proven, sets of Walschaerts valve gear to drive the wheels, rather than Gresley's conjugated motion. They were also equipped, American-style, with rocking grates and hopper ashpans below their fireboxes; these allowed fires to be dropped over pits in engine sheds, or motive power depots, a simple operation that enabled shed staff to turn the locomotives around more quickly between duties. This was also safer and less backbreaking than having to remove the fire and layers of fused coal through the firebox door as had been expected of British railway workers for generations.

Five of the last series of 'A1s' were fitted with Timken roller bearings throughout. These had previously been used on the axles of the distinctive eight-wheeled tenders of LNER Pacifics, but not on the locomotives themselves. These five engines were to prove exceptionally free running and covered significantly longer distances between major repairs than their more conventional siblings. They were also slightly more expensive to build than the main batches of 'A1s'; these cost approximately £16,000 apiece (about £350,000 in 2010), representing very good value for money. The roller bearing locomotives came in at around £18,500, much the same cost as the post-war batches of Sir William Stanier's magnificent four-cylinder 'Duchess Coronation' Pacifics, the most powerful steam locomotives built, by the LMS at its Crewe Works, for Britain's railways. The very last two, dating from 1947 and 1948, incorporating a number of US-style modifications aimed at easy maintenance, were more costly still. These were built under the direction of the last LMS CME, H. G. [George] Ivatt, son of H. A. [Henry] Ivatt, Gresley's predecessor on the Great Northern.

The 'A1s' were neither to be the fastest nor the most powerful British express passenger steam locomotives. It is possible, though, that the roller-bearing fitted 'A1s' were, at their peak – and size for size – the cheapest of all locomotives to run. Born into a post-war world, an era of austerity, fuel shortages and fears about the future, the 'A1s' were intended to be sturdy, matter-of-fact machines with just enough of the old Gresley glamour to make them win the hearts of passengers and railway managers. The reaction from enthusiasts was mixed; with such strong competition from the photogenic streamliners, coupled with the high cost of film, it is not surprising that the new order 'A1s' tended to be a little overlooked.

Fundamentally conservative in terms of design, they were no match for the last generation of US or, in particular, French steam in terms of sheer potency, thermal efficiency or modernity. They represented, however, a confident tail end of a long line of

engineering that, although modified to some extent by US and French design and practice, was descended from the Stephensons via Stirling, Ivatt and Gresley. But, the 'A1s' – averaging 118,000 miles between heavy repairs (No. 60157 *Great Eastern*, one of the engines fitted with roller bearings once clocked 190,000 miles) – came to be appreciated for their sterling service, respected perhaps more than loved.

From the start, the 'A1s' were fitted with smoke deflectors, an essential piece of kit for locomotives equipped with double Kylchap exhausts; while highly efficient, these created a notably soft blast from locomotive chimneys with the inevitable result that exhaust steam, and smoke, would trail down low over the boiler often obscuring the

In a wonderfully evocative scene showing a lost post-war world, 'A1' No. 60123 *H. A. Ivatt* passes Lincoln Central with a diverted King's Cross to Leeds and Bradford express on 1st June 1959. Named after one of the most revered Great Northern chief engineers, she was the first of the class to be withdrawn after a collision just over three years later.
JOHN P. WILSON/RAIL ARCHIVE STEPHENSON

crew's view ahead from the footplate. Smoke deflectors create an upward draft of air as the engine moves, increasing in velocity as a train accelerates, lifting exhaust steam and smoke clear of the locomotive and, just as importantly, the carriages rolling behind it. Even diehard steam enthusiasts prefer not to have cinders in their eyes or soot in their soup. One fascinating modification made to some, but not all Peppercorn 'A1s' was the fitting of silencers to the ejector exhaust pipes following complaints that these were too noisy when operating in covered stations.

As for crews, the 'A1s' were generally well-designed. As with 'A4s', both driver and firemen were provided with comfortable leather-cushioned bucket seats. Controls were all within easy reach of the driver. In their early days on the road, 'A1s' proved be hard-riding and even disturbingly uncomfortable machines compared with the smooth running 'A3s' and 'A4s'; during the design and construction of *Tornado*, this defect was corrected and, for the most part, the latest 'A1' rides like a coach.

The 'A1s' differed in terms of looks from Thompson's Pacifics in several key ways. Where Thompson moved his outside cylinders behind the front bogie, giving them a curiously naked, and clumsy, appearance, Peppercorn shifted them, Gresley-style, to the centreline of the bogies, creating a happily balanced look. Where Thompson insisted on flat-fronted cabs, Peppercorn adopted the slanting, streamlined Gresley-style, in turn adopted from earlier Chapelon Pacifics. Where Thompson's steam collecting domes on top of the boilers were curt, truncated affairs, Peppercorn favoured Gresley's elegant and racy 'Banjo-style' domes. Where Thompson's smokeboxes seem to be wobbling, with little to support them above the locomotives' buffer beams, Peppercorn's were mounted firmly and massively on far more substantial supports. Detail by detail, the Peppercorn team produced well-resolved, handsome and modern machines.

The only shortcomings were the fitting of early engines with a crude 'stovepipe' chimney, latter replaced by a traditional, and elegant, lipped design. In early BR days, 'A1s' were also marred by numberplates fixed high on their smokebox doors giving the engines a dopey appearance. This was later corrected with numberplates mounted lower down on the upper door hinge. With these in place, the 'A1s' looked modern and ever so slightly aggressive; an aesthetic that suited them well.

Straight brass nameplates were fitted to the sides of the smoke deflectors, with names spelt out in Gill Sans capitals. The lettering was slightly thicker and less elegant than the version used on the 'A4s', but still unapologetically Modern. Gills Sans, designed by Eric Gill – sculptor, letter carver, Catholic apologist and sex maniac – had been adopted wholesale by the LNER from 1929. This clear-cut type, so very different from its 'grotesque' Victorian predecessors [witnessed on the nameplates of many thousands of British locomotives], had been put into industrial production by the Monotype Corporation in 1928. The following year, Cecil Dandridge, the LNER's Advertising Manager, aiming to create a coolly modern corporate look for the railway, chose Gill Sans. Certainly, the adoption of this typeface – also used by the railway for locomotive

cabside numbers and the legend LNER emblazoned along the sides of tenders – helped give the 'A1s' a crisp, contemporary look. All told, many railwaymen as well as enthusiasts breathed a large sigh of relief when the Thompson era drew to an end and the new-look Pacifics steamed into view.

None of the new locomotives, however, was ever to work for the LNER. By the time the 'A1s' appeared, the railways had been nationalised. Peppercorn himself retired, as BR's CME Eastern and North Eastern Regions, at the end of 1949. Very sadly, he had been diagnosed as being terminally ill just a month after marrying Dorothy. She nursed him until his early death in March 1951, by which time his 'A1s' were getting into their stride.

This is what a brand new 'A1' looked like… No. 60151 (later *Midlothian*) is at Darlington on 3rd July 1949. A survivor almost to the end of the operation of the class, she still only had a working career of 16 years when more than twice that might have been anticipated.
NEVILLE STEAD COLLECTION

As no new locomotive livery, much less a logo or corporate design had been agreed at the time, the former locomotive works of the 'Big Four' tentatively turned out new engines in a semblance of old styles, and to use up pots of paint no one was willing to waste in the tough years following the end of the war.

So, the first 36 Peppercorn 'A1s' were painted LNER (or Great Northern) apple green but with the legend British Railways spelt out in full, and in capitals, along the sides of their tenders. Later on, engines were painted in the new BR standard blue designated for express passenger types. No sooner had they all been done than another policy change from 1953 saw all 49 turned out in a livery normally known as lined Brunswick green, as used by the rival Great Western Railway, but quite attractive nonetheless. Now, it was time to find out just how good the design work had been, and how the new generation 'A1s' would fare on the post-war main line.

Four East Coast Pacifics were reunited at a major crowd-pulling open day at the Barrow Hill Roundhouse working museum near Chesterfield on 4th April 2009. Compare the lines of the surviving 'A2' No. 60532 *Blue Peter* with new ' A1' No. 60163 *Tornado*. They were joined by a pair of Gresley 'A4' streamliners, Nos. 60007 *Sir Nigel Gresley* and 60009 *Union of South Africa*.
CLIVE HANLEY/A1 STEAM LOCOMOTIVE TRUST

CHAPTER THREE

On the road
Fast, but quite
a rocky ride

Pioneer production 'A1' No. 60114 *W. P. Allen* was just 16 years and four months old when she was taken out of service on Boxing Day 1964. This, at least, was more than a year above the class average. And yet, by any standards this was a wasteful use of resources. Such concerns, though, were wilfully beyond the heads of all too many railway managers and politicians at the time. A new Labour government, under Prime Minister Harold Wilson, promising a white hot technological revolution had crept into power – winning by just four seats – ten weeks before the withdrawal of No. 60114.

The fashionable talk at the time was all to do with 'modernisation', and modernisation at any cost. In 1965, the fire was dropped from the very last steam locomotive built for British Railways, the 9F 2-10-0 No. 92220 *Evening Star*; built at Swindon in 1960, this efficient and highly effective engine was barely five years old when it was discarded with only minor collision damage, unwanted by its parent region which would not sanction quite a low cost repair. This, though, was the kind of wasteful result of the railway modernisation plan announced by the British Transport Commission in December 1954 when BR's steam stock stood at 18,420. From now on, BR would be re-equipped with a fleet of new diesel and electric locomotives and trains. Steam, no matter how efficient, was to be phased out by 1970. Such was the zeal of the modernisers – technological witch-hunters – that the last official steam train on British Railways ran, ahead of schedule, in the North West of England on 11th August 1968.

Modernisation of some form had been inevitable and necessary. And, yet, it all went wrong for quite a number of years. Where BR's CME, Robin Riddles, a former assistant of Sir William Stanier and H. G. (George) Ivatt on the LMS, called for a rational phasing out of steam in favour of a predominantly electric railway network in the future, others wanted diesels, and they wanted them there and then even if the technology, in Britain at least, was undeveloped and – as it proved in the first costly diesel decade – underpowered, too slow and embarrassingly unreliable.

Perhaps the greatest performance ever recorded with a Peppercorn 'A1' came as a result of an all-too-common diesel failure in November 1958. One of the brand new English Electric Type 4 [later BR Class 40] 2,000hp diesel-electrics was unable to take the 'up' (i.e. London-bound) afternoon 'Talisman' on from York. The keen railway observer R. I. Nelson was onboard and timed the train meticulously as Driver R. Turner of King's Cross and his mate steamed out from under the great curved roof of York station, 26 minutes late. Despite six severe slowings for signals, works on the line and a complete stand at a red signal just outside King's Cross, No. 60140 *Balmoral* brought the nine-coach, 325-ton train up to a stand at the buffer stops just two and half minutes late, in 169 minutes and 12 seconds for the 188.15 miles from York. Without delays en route, the 'Talisman' would have taken just 158 minutes that day, or four minutes less than the pre-war 'Coronation' streamliner that had the advantage of passing through York without stopping.

Demonstrating the inherent efficiency of her design, *Balmoral* ran confidently up the long climb to Stevenage at 73mph and raced up into the 90s wherever possible. Down Stoke Bank near Grantham, she reached 100.5mph. What was impressive about this run

Far left: The original Peppercorn 'A1', No. 60114 *W. P. Allen*. The apple green 'Pacific' pauses in the sun in this early British railways-era scene.
T. G. HEPBURN/RAIL ARCHIVE STEPHENSON

No. 60144 *King's Courier* is already obsolete technology, as demonstrated by the diesel alongside, at King's Cross on 1st September 1962. Like many stations, King's Cross was a dark, smoky place in the days of steam.
GEOFF RIXON

was the way in which the engine ran, as far as the busy track permitted, within tight speed parameters. There was no slogging up hills; rather, *Balmoral's* driver was able to keep her up to speed, recovering time all the way, with little obvious effort. This had always been the ideal way of running long distance express trains. In France where a 75mph [120kph] speed limit, imposed by law in the 19th Century, still applied to steam locomotives in the 1960s, the aim had been to design engines that could run uphill and down at a constant 75mph, and with the heaviest of trains.

This led to the most efficient of all world steam locomotives, with machines like Andre Chapelon's '240P', '141P' and '242A1', that could run 800-ton trains at average speeds of more than 70mph by accelerating rapidly and maintaining the maximum permitted speed for as long as necessary. *Balmoral's* exploit at the head of the 'Talisman' was helped immeasurably by its French-influenced 'front end', with its free-flowing, low-pressure exhaust. Other members of the class were clocked, accurately, at three-figure speeds including No. 60125 *Scottish Union* at 102mph and our friend No. 60114 *W. P. Allen* at exactly 100mph. On several runs recorded by Cecil J. Allen (we believe no relation), the phrase "at no point was the locomotive being extended", or words to that effect, were applied to the easy performance of 'A1s'.

A 2,000hp English Electric Type 4 could never have matched *Balmoral's* performance that day, and certainly not on the day when No. 60135 *Madge Wildfire*, with 400-tons in tow, ran the 124.4 miles from Newcastle to Edinburgh Waverley in just 105 minutes at an average speed of 72mph. On another occasion, No. 60115 *Meg Merrilies* galloped from King's Cross to signals a quarter mile south of York in 150 minutes, an average of 75mph. The new diesels had neither the power to climb hills so fast nor, limited to 90mph, the speed to chase the 'A1s'. Why then, would any railway manager in their right mind have ordered 2,000hp diesels to take over from Gresley, Thompson and Peppercorn Pacifics?

The answer lies in the fact that the diesels, although unable to generate more than about 1,600 drawbar horsepower [dbhp, the power a locomotive has available to pull the train behind it; it needs the rest to move itself], were able to produce this figure more or

When the streamlined 'A4s' were introduced they were a sensation. On 7th June 1938 the crack 'West Riding Limited' from Leeds Central is well on its way to London as No. 4495 *Golden Fleece* passes Stoke signalbox and begins the dash down Stoke bank towards Peterborough.

The 'West Riding Limited' was introduced in 1937 as one of the LNER's streamlined services that epitomised this 'Golden Age' -- it was withdrawn when war broke out in 1939.

Less than a month after this picture was taken, on 3rd July 1938, sister engine No. 4468 *Mallard* tore down Stoke bank at a claimed 126mph – a world record for steam that has never been beaten.

T. G. HEPBURN/RAIL ARCHIVE STEPHENSON

less constantly, and at the turn of a handle. In 1958, and for several years to come, 1,600dbhp was quite enough to maintain time on the easy schedules laid down for express trains of the time. As Peter Townend, the innovative young shedmaster at King's Cross at the time, notes, "the changeover to diesel traction was made considerably easier because of the improvements we made to my locomotives at King's Cross; we had 'A4s' and 'A1s' capable of working diesel diagrams."

A steam locomotive of the scale of the Gresley and Peppercorn Pacifics was often designed with far more potential power than it ever normally needed. This was for several reasons. First, it was asking a lot of the fireman to shovel coal at a rate of more than 3,000lb an hour through the necessarily small firebox doors of a Pacific, especially when travelling fast and possibly bucking and swaying after tens of thousands of miles on the road after its last major service.

Second, the quality of coal could vary quite considerably in post-war years; where some coal burned brightly, relatively cleanly and with a highly effective degree of heat, other supplies might be little more than a form of low-calorific dust. This burned ineffectively leading to low boiler pressure, insufficient steam and a loss of power, while much of what the poor fireman shovelled into the firebox was simply shot up the chimney without even combusting.

Third, because tracks and signalling were not up to today's high speed standards, and, fourth, because freight trains and other slow services were often switched in front of top-flight express trains, steam locomotives needed a reserve of power to make up for lost time. There were also many more speed restrictions; for many decades, East Coast expresses had to slow to 20mph to thread a snaking path through Peterborough. Today, *Tornado* can chatter past at 75mph on the realigned straight track past the reconstructed station platforms.

On a good day, then, and with schedules as easy as the 193 minutes the diesel had that November afternoon in 1958 to run the 188.15 miles from York to King's Cross, the darlings of the modernisers had little trouble in getting by on a maximum of 2,000hp and a top speed of 90mph. All the driver had to do was to turn the handle to 'max' and leave it there until a signal flashed danger, a station hove into view, or, as often as not, something went 'phut'. It was significant that until very late in the day of steam running on BR, the Royal Train was steam-hauled whenever possible. This might well have been because the young Prince Charles was on board (The Queen and Prince Philip like steam engines, too), but, in truth, it was because of fear of diesel failure.

An 'A1' could produce, at its maximum, somewhere between 2,700 and 3,000ihp [indicated horsepower], with between 2,200 and 2,400hp available at the drawbar, that is to pull its train. These figures are way and above what could be expected of the first generation of main line British diesel locomotives. In practice, such outputs were rare. In September 1955, however, No. 60128 *Bongrace* was chosen to run test trains on the East Coast Main Line examining the new AWS [Automatic Warning System] equipment

designed to give drivers an audible warning, in the guise of klaxons and bells, of signals ahead. On one of these tests, *Bongrace* was asked to accelerate a 14-coach, 465-ton train from Grantham up to 90mph at Corby Glen three miles beyond Stoke Summit; this meant climbing up to Stoke on the way south to Peterborough as quickly as possible and then, working the engine very hard indeed, getting up to 90mph as soon as possible on the descent; accelerating rapidly from 60mph at Stoke summit to 89mph at Corby, *Bongrace* is said, by some enthusiasts, to have reached the 3,000ihp mark. Some even claimed 3,600ihp. The true figure, though, is more likely to have been around 2,800ihp.

The 3,000ihp barrier has only been crossed with certainty in Britain by a single Gresley 'A4', and by several of the Stanier 'Duchess Coronation' class Pacifics. *Mallard* herself broke a new record in 1959 when, with Driver Coe at the controls, and the highly experienced train-timer and prolific author O. S. [Oswald Stevens] Nock was on the stopwatches, she topped Stoke Bank from the south at 78mph with an 11-coach, 415-ton Newcastle express; the power required to achieve this was about 3,100ihp. In preservation, 'Duchess Coronation' No. 6233 *Duchess of Sutherland* has developed more than 3,500ihp. Significantly, these locomotives, too, were displaced by English Electric Type 4 2,000hp diesel-electrics. Equally significantly, and late in the steam day, O. S. Nock was on the footplate of the diesel-hauled 'Midday Scot' express from London Euston some time early in 1964 when the diesel's ancillary steam-boiler, providing heating for its train, failed. It was leaking water.

Off came diesel No. D332 [40132] at Crewe, to be replaced by the only spare main line locomotive available capable of tackling the formidable hills and fells beyond Preston and over Grayrigg and Shap summit to Carlisle. This was No. 46228 *Duchess of Rutland*. Eighteen minutes late away, the big red Pacific soon got into her stride with her 12-coach, 455-ton train, gaining ten minutes on the 141.1 mile run to Carlisle, in "drizzling rain", and averaging a mile-a-minute in the process. "If anyone had told me... I was about to log the fastest run I had ever experienced personally from Crewe to Carlisle", wrote Nock in his regular column in *The Railway Magazine* [June 1964], "I am afraid I should have told him not be silly! Yet so it turned out." Just like *Balmoral*, *Duchess of Rutland* had plenty of power in hand; and to reach Carlisle over those demanding hills at an average of 60mph, she only once exceeded 77mph. There had been no need to; she climbed hills with aplomb. She was withdrawn, however, full of life, in August 1964 and quickly scrapped.

Intriguingly, *Tornado*, was able to nudge a little ahead of *Duchess of Rutland* on 24th June 2010 with 'The Border Raider', a 13-coach special weighing 480 tons booked to run the 90.1 miles from Preston over Shap to Carlisle in an easy 126 minutes. In the event, *Tornado* took just 87 mins and 34 seconds, topping Shap summit at 42.5mph and, like *Duchess of Sutherland* running at 75-77mph wherever possible. The 'Duchess Coronation' had taken 90 minutes and 44 seconds for the same section with the advantage of passing through Preston without stopping, albeit at 10mph, but with the disadvantage

of being checked by signals on the approach to Carlisle. So, perhaps, the honours were even especially as the crew of the Stanier Pacific had imagined themselves sitting in the weatherproof cab of a Type 4 diesel over the snow-beaten hills to the Scottish border and were unprepared for steam. However, the sheer power of the LMS 'Duchess Coronations' has yet to be beaten in Britain: during the Second World War and with a 475-ton train, No. 6244 *King George VI* cleared Shap at 57mph. A challenge for *Tornado*.

Record runs aside, what the 'A1s' did best was to run consistently well in terms of their availability, their moderate use of coal and water and their ability to enable crews to stick to schedules day-in, day-out. Their boilers, like all LNER Pacifics, were free steaming and although heavier on coal than 'A3s' and 'A4s', firemen liked the way they kept up pressure without fuss. In his book *British Pacific Locomotives*, Cecil J. Allen published a pair of tables logging everyday runs by 'A1s' on the fast morning 'West Riding' express in the late 1950s between Hitchin and Retford. The express was allowed 96.5 minutes for the 106.7 miles, a tight schedule by the standards of the day.

Both runs demonstrate the confident ease with which the 'A1s' tacked such duties. Given a clear run, No. 60117 *Bois Roussel* reached Retford four and three-quarter minutes early. Checked by signals, and hauling an identical ten-coach train, No. 60123 *H. A. Ivatt* was nevertheless four minutes early; her net time was 87½ minutes. The logs show how quickly the 'A1s' got up to speed and how rapidly they could recover from signal checks. It's exciting today to run down the speed columns in logs by Cecil J. Allen, O. S. Nock and others (including many clergymen), and to remember just how fast steam engines could be, although largely restricted by a 90mph line limit, at the very time that the modernisation programme was doing its best to get shot of them.

It was not, in fact, until the arrival of the 3,300hp twin-engine 'Deltic' diesel-electrics [BR Class 55] from 1961, with their high-revving marine engines originally designed for motor torpedo boats, that East Coast Main Line trains could be accelerated in the way modernisers had, perhaps, intended. By this time, track and signalling had improved and the speed limit along great stretches of the East Coast Main Line raised to 100mph.

The 'Deltics', although only numbering 22 (plus a pre-production version, now preserved), were an outstanding class of diesel-electric locomotives. Weighing just 99 tons and with 3,300hp to play with, they had a high power:weight ratio and were very fast. One of them is credited with a top speed of 113mph. Named after British army regiments and racehorses, they were charismatic machines with a distinctive voice: at full speed, their high-revving opposed-piston engines sounded a bit like machine guns. The prototype was a gaudily-painted private venture locomotive sponsored by Sir George Nelson, chairman and chief executive of English Electric. The prototype 'Deltic' made a huge impression on railway engineers when put into experimental service in 1955. Neither BR operating nor board management, however, encouraged the production of further 'Deltics'; they were opposed to high-revving diesels fearing that they would be unreliable.

Tornado is a mighty machine, but it has little hope of sustaining the all out power of this one. Stanier Pacific No. 46234 *Duchess of Abercorn* from the LNER's rival, the London, Midland and Scottish Railway, climbs towards Shap summit in BR days. The 'Duchess Coronation' is passing remote Scout Green signalbox with a northbound Anglo-Scottish express.
W. J. VERDEN ANDERSON/RAIL ARCHIVE STEPHENSON

Gerard Fiennes, outspoken General Manager of BR's Eastern Region, disagreed. Effectively taking matters into his own hands, this former LNER traffic apprentice got the fleet of 'Deltics' he wanted from English Electric. Although there was talk of these replacing 55 steam Pacifics, in practice this was never the case. The 'Deltics' – built by English Electric at its Vulcan Foundry at Newton-le-Willows, Lancashire, in 1961-62 – put up very strong performances on the East Coast Main Line until their withdrawal in early January 1982. BR management, however, got its revenge when, in 1966, Fiennes published a no-holds-barred, and very entertaining, autobiography *I Tried to Run a Railway*; it earned him the sack. And, yet, Fiennes's instinct had been right. There had been no point in replacing perfectly good LNER Pacifics with not very good 2,000hp diesels. What had been needed was a quantum leap in power to make the kind of cuts to main line schedules that would have made Britain's railways competitive against motorways and inter-city jets.

Real advances only came, as Robin Riddles and others had predicted, with the full electrification of the main line from King's Cross to Edinburgh in 1991. As well as six East Coast stalwart locomotives rescued for preservation, including first-built No. D9000 [55022] *Royal Scots Grey*, the 'Deltic' engine lives on under the decks of the Royal Navy's Hunt class minesweepers, built between 1978-88.

Of all the 'A1s', the five roller-bearing fitted engines – *Flamboyant*, *Bon Accord*, *Borderer*, *Great Central* and *Great Eastern* [Nos. 60153-7] – were the star performers. In his 1961 presidential address to the Institution of Locomotive Engineers – when there were still 12,676 steam locomotives on BR's books – Freddie Harrison revealed that, in their first 12 years of service, these five engines had run a total of 4.8 million miles. One had topped a million miles in that time, an average of 228 miles every day since leaving Doncaster Works in 1949. This was exceptional going for a steam locomotive in Britain. In fact, as Harrison told his audience in Westminster, the 'A1s' as a whole had averaged 202 miles a day since new, a record for British steam. Certainly, some of their duties could be quite onerous. In April 1959, for example – and again deputising for an English Electric Type 4 diesel – No. 60156 *Great Central* took the 10am 'Flying Scotsman' from King's Cross as far as Newcastle and the 5pm back to London; it then ran the 4am to Leeds, and was at King's Cross again at 12.30pm, having run 910 miles in 30½ hours.

Given their economy, as measured by the amount of coal and water they needed to produce a given rate of drawbar horsepower an hour, and their exceptional availability – 50 per cent greater than the average British express passenger engine – Harrison went so far to declare that the 'A1s' "are, perhaps, the finest steam locomotives in the world." Comparative figures for the cost of running rival express passenger locomotives had been made between 1953-55. Where the London Midland and Scottish Regions' mighty 'Duchess Coronation' Pacifics cost an average of 12.7d [5.3 pence] per mile, and the much smaller Western Region 'Castle' class 4-6-0s cost 9.73d, the 'A1s' were clearly something of a bargain at 8.53d per mile.

The five 'A1s' fitted with roller-bearing axles were regarded as the finest development of the Peppercorn design. The first of them, York-based No. 60153 *Flamboyant*, looks in fine shape for a trip from King's Cross to Newcastle. The sturdy locomotive, in original condition with her front numberplate positioned high on the smokebox door, has just backed onto her train.

GEOFF RIXON

To bring us down to earth, and by international standards, the figures Harrison talked about so engagingly, were good, but not the best. The magnificent 6,000ihp, 100mph 'Niagara' class 4-8-4s of the Union Pacific Railroad, inspired by the CME Paul Kiefer, were clocking up between 24,000 and 28,000 miles a month (compared to a maximum of 12,200 for the 'A1s') on runs they made at the head of famous long-distance overnight expresses like the '20th Century Limited' from New York to Chicago. The Americans had made great strides with the automation of the servicing of main line steam locomotives especially in the decade following the Second World War. Big engines like the 'Niagaras', contemporaries of the 'A1s', were also mechanically stoked; no fireman could have met the demands of a fire grate twice the area of an 'A1'. And yet, the US steam locomotives were doomed, too. The diesel lobby had made its case earlier than in Britain and, for better or worse, it had won the day – and the American railroads. Before the 'A1s' were finally taken out service in 1966, however, not even the new diesels could save passenger services on US railroads: jet aircraft had taken over.

If the railways had not been nationalised and Harrison had, in due course, replaced Peppercorn as CME of the LNER, he would, he said, have continued to develop the steam locomotive for the East Coast Main Line. Gresley had wanted to build a three-cylinder 4-8-2, a design on the Doncaster drawing boards in 1939. Tentative outline designs had also been drawn up for a streamlined and conventional three-cylinder 4-8-4. What Harrison really wanted to build, though, was a four-cylinder compound 4-8-2 with a marine-style water tube boiler pressed to 400psi. It would have been far more powerful than a 'Deltic' diesel and, undoubtedly, a stirring machine. Might the A1 Steam Locomotive Trust be attempted to realise Harrison's dream?

Harrison went on to carry the Gresley torch into BR days. As one of the four regional Chief Mechanical and Electrical Engineers, he was given the opportunity to play a major part in the design of a new three-cylinder Pacific at Derby. The chance arose when, on 8th October 1952, a terrible accident at Harrow & Wealdstone station on the West Coast Main Line just north of Euston, that cost many lives, also witnessed the destruction of No. 46202 *Princess Anne*. This was a brand new four-cylinder Pacific rebuilt from the Stanier Turbomotive, an experimental turbine-driven engine of 1935. Riddles commissioned a prototype of a new BR Standard express passenger Pacific as a replacement for *Princess Anne*. The design was essentially Harrison's with input from E. S. 'Stuart' Cox and C. S. Cocks, Harrison's chief draftsman at Derby.

Harrison and his team created a superb-looking modern locomotive, This was British Railways '8P' 4-6-2 No. 71000 *Duke of Gloucester* (originally suggested to have been named *Prince of Wales*, but Buckingham Palace was not supportive), which was completed in April 1954. It combined Stanier's work with a generous dash of Gresley. A three-cylinder Pacific with Caprotti valve gear, *Duke of Gloucester* was the most efficient of all British locomotives measured by its ability to use steam economically.

Sadly, No. 71000 never lived up to her potential in BR days. This was partly because work on steam locomotive development in Britain was grinding to a halt, but also because a number of manufacturing faults had remained uncorrected and were to remain so until 2010, by which time the last defects on the beautifully restored Pacific had been corrected. Equally, conservative design traditions, despite Harrison's protests, led to such short-sighted instructions from on top that No. 71000 must be fitted with a conventional double blastpipe and chimney and not a superbly efficient double Kylchap exhaust that would have made the locomotive considerably more potent than she proved to be in everyday service.

Today, with a new Kylchap exhaust, a modified ashpan to assist with draughting and a properly aligned middle cylinder, 'The Duke' demonstrates just how well a new generation of steam locomotives might and should have performed from the mid-1950s until a comprehensive electrification of the railways had been completed. Her limitation, even today, is her boiler which is simply too small, or otherwise unable, to keep up with the demand for steam at the 'front end'. All those many, various and unreliable diesel-electrics and diesel-hydraulic locomotives Harrison had to deal with when he took over from Riddles, as BR's CME, in 1958 – they were already on order and there was little he could do to stem the initial oily flow – would have been unnecessary if perhaps 'The Duke' had been properly sorted, and a new generation of steam locomotives had been able to hold diesels at bay until the electrics were ready to take over.

The 'A1s' helped the new diesels until they were effectively banned on the southern stretches of the East Coast Main Line. Keith Farr (*Steam World*, November 1998) recalls

working at the enquiry office at King's Cross over the Easter holiday in 1964. "I thought I had seen my last 'A1s' in revenue earning service, at any rate south of Peterborough ... Suddenly a voice announced, "there's a steamer on the 'Yorkshire Pullman'. I glanced at the television screen summarising the progress of 'up' expresses; sure enough steam had replaced a failed diesel at Doncaster, but what was this? It was regaining time on the (admittedly easy) 'Deltic' schedule. Once again 'The Cross' echoed to Kylchap song as the 'Yorkshire Pullman' drew to a stand in 150 minutes for the 156 miles from Doncaster ... as *W. P. Allen* backed out, to vanish in the murk of Gasworks tunnel, with a plaintive note on that high-pitched whistle, I wondered whether I would ever again see steam at King's Cross or an 'A1' in action."

If the 'A1s' had an Achilles' heel, especially in their early days, it was their notorious rough riding at speed and so much so that many drivers hated having to take them above 80mph. The cause of this appears to have been a mystery for some long while. In a letter to the railway historian Colonel H. C. B. Rogers, Peter Townend, then Assistant District Motive Power Superintendent, King's Cross, wrote "Some of the 'A1s' at King's Cross gave rise to complaints of bad riding. At that time we had 12 allocated, along with 19 'A4s' and eleven 'A3s'. The worst individual locomotive at the time was No. 60157 *North Eastern*, fitted with roller bearings. The engine oscillated from side to side on straight track as soon as you reached 60mph... the locomotive 'crabbed' its way along straight track, with a lateral movement of the engine/tender fall plate of about 12 inches."

This would have been alarming as well as making it almost impossible to fire the engine. Swinging a shovel laden with coal from the tender of a speeding 'A1' through the fire doors and on to a white hot grate is difficult enough at walking speed; at 60mph, while 'crabbing', it must have been beyond the capability of any normal young man. Crews at King's Cross in the 1950s were allocated a specific engine; many requested transfers from 'A1s' to 'A4s'. But, as Townend explains, crews could be a fickle lot. "Many of the crews at King's Cross had regular engines and preferred 'A4s' for the ride and general comfort. Two crews shared an 'A1', No. 60156 *Great Central*, all the time it was at King's Cross and did not want anything else. Another driver would not take an 'A1' in place of his usual 'A4' because it was draughty and he had a bad back! I do not think the shed staff had any special opinions about them, however, as they were given their jobs without any preferences". All agreed, however, that the 'A1s' were lighter on maintenance. "Overall", says Townend, "the 'A1s', in terms of power, overall costs, steaming and general reliability were well in front of everything else on the other railways."

The reputation for rough riding, however, was to haunt the 'A1s' as well as trying the nerves, and backs, of crews. Dr Patrick Ransome-Wallis, a Herne Bay doctor who travelled extensively on railways and locomotive footplates around the world, and wrote about them in entertaining books, took his first ride on an 'A1' south from Newcastle in 1955. The train was the 'Flying Scotsman', all 13 coaches and 510 tons of it, and the engine, an immaculate No. 60150 *Willbrook*. As speed rose to 50mph, Ransome-Wallis noted, "These great engines have a habit of 'waggling their tails' in a sharp side to side movement, very like that of the old Great Northern Atlantics, and they are nothing like so comfortable on the footplate at speed as are the 'A4s'." O. S. Nock noted, "the only time I have been really scared on a footplate of a steam locomotive was on one of these engines working a Birmingham-Glasgow express over the Caledonian line between Carlisle and Beattock."

Everyone seems to agree that while the engines steamed extremely well – pressure allowed to drop to 150 lb/sq in at stations could be raised very quickly to 250lb/sq in once on the move – their ride was a little too exciting for comfort, even in the bump and grind era of Rock 'n' Roll. Later on, it was discovered that the front four-wheeled bogie beneath the cylinders and smokebox, had been designed, with precious little modification, for Thompson's altogether smaller and lighter two-cylinder mixed-traffic 'B1' 4-6-0s and with too few modifications for the much larger and heavier 'A1s'. Because it was too light for the 'A1s', and the control springs checking lateral movement were effectively too soft, the 'B1'-derived bogies ran ragged under the Pacifics; they were unable to centre the chassis on straight tracks at speed. You can see this effect in action on any number of model locomotives racing around electric train sets whereby the front bogie wobbles about while the driving wheels do all the work. When new side control springs were added, or when the bogies were replaced by the version used on the 'A4s', the riding of the 'A1s' was vastly improved, although this was never up to the standard set by Gresley.

The Peppercorn 'A1s' were not designed to run the sort of fast streamlined trains that had gained maximum and well-deserved publicity for the pre-war LNER. Altogether

In steam days the departure of a train from a great terminus was a dramatic event. 'A1' No. 60121 *Silurian* powers away from King's Cross with a train to Newcastle on 18th August 1962.
GEOFF RIXON

more matter-of-fact than Gresley's celebrated 'A4s', they nevertheless provided much of the backbone of East Coast Main Line services in the 1950s and into the early 1960s. In early post-war days – the years of Austerity and rationing – the 'A1s' were asked to pull long, heavy trains at moderate speeds. As O. S. Nock recalled, " I remember so well a running superintendent making a comparison thus wise: 'the Gresleys are the greyhounds of the service, but if you have to take 600 tons on a dirty night give me a Peppercorn every time'."

Although built too late to take part in the 1948 Locomotive Exchanges that witnessed 'A4s' competing with Great Western 'Kings' and LMS 'Duchess Coronations' in what proved to be an unsatisfactory, and rather half-hearted attempt, to find the ideal express passenger locomotives for future service on BR, a test made between the 'A1s' and 'A2s' was conducted in spring 1949. The first of the double chimney 'A2s', No. 60539 *Bronzino* was put up against No. 60114 *W. P. Allen.* The results proved little, however, as the two locomotives were by and large identical. Comparisons made with statistics from the 1948 Locomotive Exchanges were interesting in that while the large grates of the Peppercorn Pacifics made these locomotives hungrier for coal at medium power outputs, when it came to slogging, as they were sometimes asked to do with test trains weighing up to 600 tons, they proved to be slightly more economical than the 'A4s'. All this, though, was rather marginal information. Of more use, both Pacifics were found to be powerful with the 'A2' producing a maximum of 2,138dbhp at 63.2 mph and the 'A1', 2,108dbhp at 61.2mph; although capable of greater performances than these, the tests did show that the 'A1s' would be the reliably strong engines needed at time of economic hardship, and long, heavy main line trains. They were not designed to be racehorses like the 'A4s', but sturdy slogging hunters for BR's Eastern, North Eastern and Scottish Region main lines.

What the locomotives were capable of in such conditions was soon proved in early performance logs published in *The Railway Magazine*. A 1950 log shows No. 60115 *Meg Merriles*, with driver Archie Waugh of Gateshead, and weighed down with a 13-coach, 495-ton train, running the 162.8 miles from Newcastle to Grantham in 163 minutes and, the process, cutting 20 minutes off the current schedule.

For several spells between 1951 and 1953, three 'A1s' – Nos. 60152 *Holyrood*, 60160 *Auld Reekie* and 60161 *North British* – were loaned to Polmadie shed, Glasgow, where they worked a number of sleeping car and 'postal' expresses over Beattock to Carlisle and even further south over Shap to Crewe. Cecil J. Allen was onboard a 12-coach train weighing 420 tons in 1952. "The running", he wrote, "was well up to average 'Duchess' standards and Beattock was passed in an actual time of 40 min 50 sec or in 39 ½ net for the 39.7 miles".

As the 1950s accelerated into a new age of economic boom and consumerism, so long distance and other express trains changed with them. By the end of the decade, there were far fewer 600-ton trains slogging and up and down the East Coast route and far more lightweight expresses, often of no more than nine coaches, sprinting – inter-city style – at diesel speeds behind steam Pacifics. It was then that the big grates of the 'A1s', and the need for these to be covered with coal, could be seen as an example of over-engineering. Even so, the 'A1s' could run fast when asked to and they were, without doubt, reliable locomotives as well – as the cheapest of all British Pacifics to run.

At first, the Peppercorn 'A1s' were very much English engines, with few being allocated north of the border. This was to change over the years and especially as diesels pushed the 'A1s' away from crack expresses over the old Great Northern route to London. Their purposeful performance, however, proved to be a shield against earlier dieselisation. The LNER had, in fact, been thinking of commissioning pairs of 1,600hp diesel-electrics to run main line express from 1947; the 'A1s', however, did all that might have been required of such diesels and at a much lower capital cost.

Somehow the 'A1s', for all their slightly menacing good looks, never caught the imagination of railway enthusiasts as a whole, in the way the elegant 'A3s' and charismatic 'A4s' did. It was, perhaps, only in their last days that it dawned on many enthusiasts just how special the 'A1s' really were. They had been the main line chorus to the Gresley soloists, but after relative celebrity No. 60123 *H. A. Ivatt* was condemned after a collision while hauling the fast 7.15pm London to Leeds goods train on 7th September 1962 and the 'A1s' began to leave the stage.

And, this despite the fact that several of the class, in generally excellent condition, had been fitted with brand new boilers during 1961, the latest – No. 60120 *Kittiwake* – that August. *Kittiwake* was taken out of service in January 1964 after a smash and scrapped soon after at Darlington Works where *Tornado* was to be built. Two of the engines – No. 60124 *Kenilworth* and No. 60145 *Saint Mungo* – hung on, on pilot duty at Darlington and Newcastle, although with increasingly less work to do as diesel breakdowns finally dropped with the arrival of the competent Brush Type 4 [Class 47] 2,750hp all-purpose diesel-electrics from 1962. The very last 'A1' in service, No. 60145 *Saint Mungo*, was finally laid aside on 19th June 1966. As late as 31st December 1965 she had been logged on an express running south from Darlington; with just eight coaches in tow, *Saint Mungo* covered 43.5 miles to a signal stop outside York in 38 minutes and 45 seconds, reaching a tantalising 99mph on level track. She was hardly ready for scrap.

The desire to rid the railways of steam, however, had not been a rational one, even if this was the way it had been presented. Modernisation was as much about image as commonsense. And, yet, increasingly voices began to be heard by enthusiasts as well as that almost extinct breed of engineers committed to steam, questioning the dubious logic of replacing steam so very quickly in favour of an expensive form of motive power that was not even cheap to run. A letter from Robert W. Jackson, of Sheffield, published in *The Railway Magazine* for November 1968 is worth quoting in full. It was the voice of commonsense, and of steam:

"The typical characteristics of modern transport equipment are capital intensiveness and short life expectancy. Consequently the required break-even annual earning power

More than a century of hands-on steam experience: Former King's Cross shedmaster Peter Townend (left) shares his memories with Dick Hardy on a 2008 'Talisman' special along the East Coast Main Line. Dick held a variety of senior engineering positions across both Eastern and Southern territories, and both are published authors on good steam practice.
HOWARD JOHNSTON

is considerable, especially considering modern interest rates of seven or eight per cent. Diesel traction gives typical examples of these characteristics. A diesel costs roughly two-and-a-half times to construct than the steam engine it replaces, and while the average age of some 200 steam locomotives withdrawn in 1957 I have worked out to be 49, the average age of 169 diesels withdrawn earlier this year was 9.5.

"Eliminating temporarily interest and depreciation, an engine costing two-and-a-half times more and lasting a fifth as long needs an annual earning capacity (that is, receipts/operating costs) of greater than 12.5 times that of its rival in order to be a better commercial proposition. If a good diesel in favourable circumstances does the work of two-and-a-half modern steam engines and has operating costs per mile down to half those of a steamer, then these savings clearly go nowhere near the observed dissavings of high costs and short life. Furthermore, the choice in recent years has often been between persevering with existing steam engines for, say, ten or 15 years and replacing them with diesels lasting the same length of time. Interest foregone, compounded at about seven per cent for 15 years, must therefore be included as a cost of dieselisation. For example, I

The first Peppercorn 'A1' to be withdrawn, No. 60123 *H. A. Ivatt* at Doncaster on 29th September 1962, after it was damaged in an accident at Offord. It was never repaired.
GAVIN MORRISON

estimate the total cost (excluding depreciation) 1961–76 of running annually 4.3 million miles of East Coast expresses is up to £8.8 million by the 50 'A1' class Pacifics or at least £12.41 million by the 22 'Deltics'. How then does dieselisation pay its way?"

Those 22 'Deltics' never did replace the 49 'A1s'; however proficient, they were backed up by legions of, at first, 2,000hp English-Electric Type 4s and, increasingly, by 2,750hp Brush Type 4s [Class 47] from the mid-1960s. As for engine crews, the debate was often more visceral than intellectual. As Peter Townend says, "There was a lot of desire to keep the much improved tried-and-tested steam locomotives as they were mostly driven by senior men who, whilst trained on the new diesels were not happy or confident to overcome their failures. However, at some depots, crews objected if the diesel was replaced by a steam engine because they had no overalls and, of course, there was not the dirt and general discomfort on their new steeds." Townend adds, "Enthusiasts cheer on the 'Deltics', but the noise and fumes were awful!" What was certain was that even as they were withdrawn from service, the Peppercorn Pacifics had years of fast, powerful and reliable life left in them.

Two superstars in one flying formation… 'A1' No. 60163 *Tornado* was a magnificently appropriate choice to escort record-breaking 'A4' No. 4468 *Mallard* up the East Coast Main Line from its usual home at the National Railway Museum at York to the annexe at Shildon on 24th June 2010.
STEVE PHILPOTT/A1 STEAM LOCOMOTIVE TRUST

CHAPTER FOUR

Out of steam
But not for very long!

The last official steam-hauled train on British Railways ran on 11th August 1968. This was the famous 'Fifteen Guinea Special', an expensive trip at the time, taking its lucky, if mournful, passengers from Liverpool to Manchester and on to Carlisle and back. The locomotives for different sections of the run werethree Stanier 'Black Five' 4-6-0s – the Jeeps of the main-line railways – and No. 70013 *Oliver Cromwell*, a gleaming Brunswick green BR Standard 'Britannia' class Pacific, the last main line BR locomotive to have been overhauled at Crewe in February 1967. Starting the next day, steam was banned from the main line.

Had the modernisers finally triumphed? Very nearly, but not quite. The fires may have been quenched in locomotives of the regular BR fleet, yet steam just managed to carry on regardless of the blanket ban imposed on it. First, there was the Vale of Rheidol Railway, the narrow-gauge line climbing from the Cambrian coast at Aberystwyth to picturesque Devil's Bridge, and powered, as it always had been, by the old order. Not only was the line worked by steam, but some witty (or was it dutiful?) soul had the rather brilliant idea of repainting the locomotives and their trains in the latest corporate blue-and-white Inter-City livery complete with BR's striking new logo. This was an Inter-Village, rather than Inter-City route, but what a delight it was to see the Vale of Rheidol's vintage steam trains cocking a snook at steam-hating management miles down the line in London.

The Vale of Rheidol carried on under BR ownership until 1989, when. ahead of the main lines, it was privatised. It had been the most unlikely outpost of BR steam working hard

The 'first' and the 'last'? No.60163 *Tornado* simmers at Loughborough, Great Central Railway, on 10th October 2008, along with 'Britannia' No. 70013 *Oliver Cromwell*. The BR-built 'Brit' hauled British Rail's last standard gauge steam train on 11th August 1968 and was subsequently saved for the nation. It returned to the main line after a campaign by the magazine *Steam Railway*.
PHIL METCALFE

to please the summer crowds after the August 1968 ban. There was, though, one other chink in BR's modern armour. *Flying Scotsman*. Probably the world's most famous steam locomotive, No. 60103 *Flying Scotsman* (perhaps better known as No. 4472) had been withdrawn from BR Eastern Region service in January 1963 after a long and highly distinguished career. She was bought for £3,000 by Alan Pegler, a colourful industrialist, ex-RAF bomber pilot, former member of the Eastern Area Board of BR and President of the Ffestiniog Railway in North Wales, a line he did much to revive in the 1950s.

Cleverly, Pegler signed an agreement with BR allowing him to run *Flying Scotsman* on the main line until 1971. In doing so, he came to beat the ban. Back in steam that year, *Flying Scotsman* brought a brilliant streak of colour and glamour into what had survived of the largely run-down main line steam railway. On 1st May 1968, the 'A3' made news headlines when she re-enacted, 40 years on, the first non-stop run of the 'Flying Scotsman' express from King's Cross to Edinburgh. At a time when there were very few opportunities left to travel long distance by steam in Britain, this was a brilliant occasion, and caught for posterity on film by the BBC. Films and photographs recording *Flying Scotsman's* thunderous departure from King's Cross that day are deeply enjoyed today.

A 'Deltic'-hauled diesel express paced alongside the Gresley Pacific before accelerating ahead of her, with a sense that here was the new world overtaking the old. And yet today it is *Flying Scotsman* that has sped on into the 21st Century, attracting crowds and wooing the media. The 'Deltics', for all their undoubted prowess (these were the most impressive of the BR diesel-electric locomotives, designed to replace Gresley, Thompson and Peppercorn Pacifics) have all but vanished. Ultimately, *Flying Scotsman* had more staying power than an early-1960s 3,300hp diesel-electric.

In the 1960s, after its purchase from BR by Alan Pegler, *Flying Scotsman* became ever more famous and toured the country on special trains. In 1967 the Gresley machine is near Newtown Harcourt, south of Leicester, with a charter working from London's St Pancras.
BRIAN STEPHENSON

Flying Scotsman, built in 1923 for the LNER, had been a favourite engine right from the moment she stepped onto the railway. She was put on display at the British Empire Exhibition held at Wembley in 1924, and again in 1925. Equipped with one of Gresley's ingenious corridor tenders – designed so crews could change en route without the train having to stop – she ran non-stop from London to Edinburgh on 1st May 1928 and was the locomotive many passengers travelling on the famous 'Flying Scotsman' express, the 10am from King's Cross, hoped to see at the head of their prestigious train. She starred, the following year, in *Flying Scotsman*, the first British film documentary boasting sound. In 1934, *Flying Scotsman* became the first British locomotive to reach an authenticated 100mph. By the 1960s, in her smart BR uniform, and equipped with several modifications to improve steaming, not least a Kylchap exhaust and a pair of German-style smoke deflectors attached to the smokebox, the celebrated Gresley Pacific was running better than ever.

Pegler's ambitious adventures with *Flying Scotsman* sadly led to bankruptcy. He had taken the locomotive to the United States in 1969, but the trip – quite a riotous affair by all accounts, much like a heavy metal rock band on tour – had become all too expensive to manage. Luckily, in 1973 the itinerant Pacific was bought by William McAlpine and returned home. *Flying Scotsman* set off for Australia next. This was in 1988. She clocked up an impressive 28,000 miles down under, and claimed a world record for steam by running non-stop over the 422 miles from Parkes to Broken Hill in New South Wales. On her way back to Britain, she also became the first, and perhaps the only, steam locomotive to have travelled – partly by rail, partly by sea – around the world.

Bought, at auction, by the National Railway Museum in April 2004 – with financial support from Heritage Lottery Fund, Virgin billionaire Richard Branson, Yorkshire Forward and a public appeal – *Flying Scotsman* has been undergoing a painstaking restoration, with a return to the main line scheduled, aged 88, in 2011. What *Flying Scotsman*, and her extraordinary story, did from 1968 until the beginning of a return to steam on the main line in October 1971, was to keep the steam lobby's hopes up. To railway management of the time, steam was dirty, old-fashioned and detrimental to the image of a modern railway. They were wrong. Hundreds of thousands of people in Britain – millions even – love steam locomotives. The sight, sound and steamy adventures of *Flying Scotsman* helped thaw the ice between public desire and BR's refusal to look a steam locomotive in its firebox door. In October 1971 the ice broke, and the Great Western four-cylinder 4-6-0 No. 6000 *King George V* pulled a passenger steam train on the main line.

Quite how this happened is a matter of conjecture. The fact that there had been a change of government might have helped. In 1970, Harold Wilson's Labour government was voted out of office in favour of the Tories under Edward Heath. Although Heath's Conservative government was still keen on the notion of modernisation, it was also dependent to an extent on the goodwill of big business; *King George V* owed her new lease of life to H.P. Bulmer, the cider company based in Hereford.

When many of its sisters had already been withdrawn, 'A1' No. 60124 *Kenilworth* was enjoying a final visit to Darlington Works on 9th May 1964. This is where many of the class were constructed, although No. 60124 was a Doncaster product. She survived in service until March 1966.

F. COULTON

There is no glory left for one of the most popular 'A1s' with a classic name. Split away from her tender, No. 60158 *Aberdonian* is already partly dismantled in the Hughes Bolckow scrapyard in early 1965.

K. HUDSPETH

No more express work for this sad-looking 'A1', and this is the brutal end that awaited all the original Peppercorn 'A1s'. Heaton, Tweedmouth and Gateshead shed were all home to No. 60116 *Hal o'The Wynd* before a final journey was made to Hughes Bolckow of Blyth for evisceration in the summer of 1965.
B. ANDERSON

When the end came, 'A1s' were sold the highest bidder, and the Hughes Bolckow scrapyard in Blyth was the recipient of several East Coast Pacifics. 'A1s' Nos. 60142 *Edward Fletcher* and 60116 *Hal o'The Wynd* wait with another unidentified locomotive to be broken up for scrap on 5th August 1965.
I. SPENCER

Bulmers placed adverts in the railway press in the course of 1969 to explain what they were up to. "Why are Bulmers – the World's largest cider makers – playing at trains?" asked the adverts. The answer was telling in the light of *Tornado's* hugely successful public debut forty years down the line. "Somebody has told our Managing Director that there are two million railway enthusiasts and he thinks that by restoring a famous locomotive to working order he may persuade these two million people absolutely to insist on Bulmer's cider and not just anybody's cider." In other words, not only was there an enormous number of steam enthusiasts in Britain, despite BR's desperate attempt to denigrate the steam locomotive and to ban it from its tracks in favour of diesels guzzling oil from the politically-sensitive Middle East, but there was a big market out there to be tapped.

It is difficult to say with anything like scientific certainty exactly how many railway enthusiasts switched from pints of foaming Bass and Double Diamond to tankards of sweet sparkling Strongbow and Woodpecker from 1969, yet here was an advertising agency's dream, a strong, identifiable and enthusiastic market. It would be some decades, however, before the steam 'business' moved away from being the stuff of duffel bags, baggy trousers, Ilford Sportman cameras and fish paste sandwiches to one that could be indulged with Pullman dining on long-distance, main line steam specials, let alone seduced by the unmitigated luxury of trains like the 'Orient Express'.

At the time, steam's horizon seemed distinctly limited. As those Bulmers ads stated: "From time to time the engine [*King George V*] will steam on the three-quarters of a mile of private track" of the cider maker's Hereford factory. Hereford to Paddington and beyond seemed quite out of the question in 1969. The Bulmers, though, were well-connected, and it is not difficult to imagine talks behind the scenes, over brandy and cigars, between businessmen, politicians and sympathetic railway executives, about what fun it would be to let some steam back on the main lines. In any case, that arch-moderniser and professional rationalist Dr Richard Beeching had done his job and gone into retirement, and the even the most ardent modernisers were beginning to calm down. Whatever the truth, the ban ended up lasting just over three years. Steam was back.

Not that it was plain steaming of course. It took a while for steam owners and operators to prove they could guarantee reliable, efficient services able to conform to ever-increasing rules and regulations laid down for a safe railway. For several years, all main line steam locomotives were restricted to a maximum of 60mph. It was only when this limit was raised to 75mph, for locomotives with driving wheels 6ft 2in and over, that long-distance steam excursions hauled by powerful and fleet-footed Pacifics began to make sense.

What Alan Pegler and *Flying Scotsman* had done was to lay the tracks for today's impressive line-up of main line Pacifics running heavy trains at schedules demanding, on occasion, mile-a-minute timings. If anyone had suggested this in 1968, they would have been thought either too romantic for their own good, or even a little mad. Steam had been all but wiped out between 1955-68 at a rate that must have satisfied even Dr Beeching, BR's ruthlessly modernising chairman brought in from ICI to take an axe to the railways.

Beeching's *Reshaping of British Railways* report of 1963 (a book that never carried his name even once) led to the closure of over 4,000 route miles, or 25 per cent of that year's total, over the next decade along with the closure of 3,000, or half of all stations. Countless branch lines vanished (railway enthusiasts could count them, of course), along with the thousands of small steam locomotives that had operated them with bucolic charm for so many decades. Even main lines were closed, including the former Great Central after which one of the five roller-bearing fitted 'A1s' was named. Others were dieselised, some electrified. Steam locomotives, many in their prime, were dumped in queues outside motive power depots or else dragged to scrapyards up and down the country. It seemed impossible that, by the first week of August 1968, all 18,000 listed in 1955 had gone.

For most steam locomotives there was no escape from the military-style disposal system that had to be implemented because railway works were swamped with engines being condemned, often at the rate of a couple of hundred a month. As well as being a problem of space, the expanding national economy of the 1960s required sources of high quality materials. The closure of so many routes coupled to the thinning out of the assets on what survived yielded immense quantities of rails, wagons, coaches and of course steam locomotives. Although often difficult to render down and separate, the wealth of copper and brass to be recovered made disposal a lucrative business for private contractors. When export restrictions were briefly lifted in 1959, almost a million tonnes of metal went to overseas furnaces as distant as India and Japan.

The 'A1s' were all caught up in the meltdown and, with a single exception sold to a South Wales scrap dealer, every locomotive from the fleet created by the London & North Eastern Railway was quickly liquidated. The sole escapee was a 'B1' 4-6-0 designed by Edward Thompson but delivered from the North British Locomotive Company's Glasgow Works in December 1947 when his successor Arthur Peppercorn was in office. It ended up in the scrapyard owned by Woodham Brothers in Barry, South Wales. This particular yard was to become, by default and happy accident, a Mecca for steam enthusiasts, and one of the most important triggers for the steam revival on Britain's main line railways.

Dai Woodham had come back from serving in the Royal Artillery in Italy during the Second World War looking to expand his father's business. By the mid-1950s, Woodham Brothers were doing a healthy trade in high quality scrap metal selling this on to the newly-nationalised steel industry. When BR modernised, Woodham Brothers began scrapping thousands of old four-wheeled coal wagons. Although Woodham began buying ex-Great Western locomotives for scrap in 1959, so many wagons arrived at the marshalling yards Dai Woodham had leased at Barry, that there was little time to cut up the steam locomotives. They would take longer to take apart, so they were laid aside for a rainy day.

By August 1968, Woodham had bought a total of 297 steam locomotives, of which 213 were eventually sold on to preservation groups. Woodham always claimed to have had no sentimental attachment to the locomotives lined up in droves at Barry; even so, he allowed buyers to put down a deposit to secure a particular engine and to settle up whenever they could. The list of locomotives rescued from Barry for preservation is almost breathtaking. Thumbing down, it is possible to spot two Great Western 'King' 4-6-0s, four 'Castles', 17 'Halls', eight 'Manors', a pair of Stanier three-cylinder 'Jubilee' 4-6-0s, seven BR Standard '9F' 2-10-0s, ten ex-Southern Region Bulleid 'Merchant Navy' Pacifics, no fewer than eighteen Bulleid 'West Country' and 'Battle of Britain' light Pacifics, BR's last express engine No. 71000 *Duke of Gloucester* and just the one ex-LNER locomotive, a Thompson 'B1' mixed traffic 4-6-0 No. 61264.

The Barry locomotives provide the backbone of the fleet of main line steam locomotives in Britain today. Many locomotive types were missing of course – including an 'A1'.

The whole story might have been completely different had a bid, by Geoff Drury, a businessman who later went on to buy the 'A4' No. 60019 *Bittern*, succeeded in saving final survivor No. 60145 *Saint Mungo*. His attempt failed, and the 'A1' was sent to Drapers of Hull for cutting up in August 1966. Drury did manage to buy the next best thing, the last working Peppercorn 'A2', No. 60532 *Blue Peter* (withdrawn on 31st December 1966), so at least there was a modern LNER Pacific to look at. Funds to help save the locomotive were partly raised by BBC Television's highly popular *Blue Peter* show. The combination was a guaranteed success; when the show's presenters, Val Singleton, Peter Purves and John Noakes, turned up at Doncaster Works in November 1970 to rename the newly-restored No. 60532, freshly repainted in non-authentic but attractive LNER apple green (it was constructed under the aegis of British Railways) they were met by a crowd 60,000 strong.

Today, six 'A4s', one 'A3' and one 'A2' survive. No Thompson Pacific escaped the scrapyards, and there seem to be few regrets. The Barry experience, meanwhile, had been doubly important to the revival of British steam because the official list of locomotives, drawn up in 1961, to be preserved for the nation had always seemed meagre and patchy. To a number of enthusiasts it was apparent that steps needed to be taken quickly to save locomotives, and indeed trains, missing from the official list. A group of sixteen-year-old Middlesex schoolboys led by Graham Parry began campaigning that year to save a classic Great Western '14XX' 0-4-2 tank locomotive and one of the 'auto-coaches', these small yet characterful and extremely fast engines were still chasing along branch lines Dr Beeching had yet to axe. Their energetic and foresighted attempt to do something against the official grain led to the formation of the Great Western Society, one of the lynchpins of the steam preservation movement, and based today at a fully-working 1930s engine shed at Didcot, Oxfordshire. Using parts recycled from duplicated Barry types, the GWS is currently building a Hawksworth 'County' 4-6-0 and a Churchward 'Saint' 4-6-0, two classes that became extinct before anyone thought of preserving them.

Even before the 1961 national list, the Bluebell Railway had opened. This was the world's first preserved standard gauge steam railway, running, from August 1960, between Horsted Keynes and Sheffield Park in Sussex on a stretch of the East Grinstead to Lewes line that had closed in March 1958. Today, the Bluebell's collection ranks second only in number to the national collection at the National Railway Museum, York; a replica of

Beachy Head, a Marsh 'H2' Atlantic [4-4-2] is under construction at Sheffield Park, installing a rediscovered boiler onto a set of brand new frames and wheels. The original locomotive was only a slight variation on H. A. Ivatt's large-boilered Atlantic for the GNR, the influence of which can also be detected in the design of *Tornado*.

Unofficial steam preservation in Britain, though, had really started with those narrow-gauge railways in Wales during the era of austerity and ration books. The first of these captivating railways to be taken over by enthusiasts was the Talyllyn in 1951; in fact, this was the first railway in the world to be run by amateurs. These narrow-gauge railways are important in the story of main line preservation, for they allowed enthusiasts to build up the experience of running railways, raising funds, restoring locomotives and facing up to safety and other legislation that would determine whether or not they were allowed to take steam on into the future. They also learned much about publicity and marketing as well as goodwill. Sixty years ago, railways like the Talyllyn would have seemed remote and exotic to most people in Britain; today they are very popular indeed.

One of those involved in the Welsh narrow-gauge steam world was, of course, Alan Pegler. It was Pegler who funded the first enthusiasts on the Ffestiniog Railway in 1954; the railway re-opened to passenger traffic the following year. By 1963, Pegler was ready and prepared to take on a full-blooded, 100mph standard gauge Pacific and, in 1968, to run it non-stop from London to Edinburgh just as BR was ridding itself of its very last steam locomotives.

Pegler and *Flying Scotsman* proved that privately preserved main line steam was a realistic proposition. And, then, when *King George V* steamed onto the main line again in 1971, things began to click. The experience, confidence and sheer desire to see steam back where it belonged drove a freshly-motivated preservation movement on to new and more exacting challenges than before. Railway managers themselves began to relax. Steam was clearly popular and, remarkably, proved it had an appeal for younger generations and not just for those born before the 1955 Modernisation Plan. Steam locomotives, many began to realise, could be good ambassadors for the railways; they made people feel good about them. The media liked them, too, although all too many newspapers along with radio and television broadcasters tended to cast them in a 'Thomas the Tank Engine' role, referring to any steam locomotive as an old-time 'chuff-chuff'. An 'A1' at full chat with 500 tons of train and more behind it sounds nothing like an antiquated 'puffer' train – it sounds purposeful and thrilling, more like an aero engine.

In the 1990s, the privatisation of Britain's railways – a hurriedly engineered move in the dying days of Prime Minister John Major's first Conservative government, was to prove one of the greatest friends to the steam preservation business. Although this was a controversial (and largely dim-witted) measure, it allowed railway operators more or less free access to the main line network. If a company could offer a new high-speed diesel or electric service, then why not steam? As long as operators were able to prove that their trains could cope safely with the modern railway network and fit, one way or another, its timetables, then there was no valid legal reason to keep steam off the tracks.

By 2010, the sheer number of steam trains running on the main line in Britain, many to exacting schedules, would have seemed impossible to those riding or watching the 'Fifteen Guinea Special' steam past on 11th August 1968.

Not all railway managers had moved on from the modernising zeal that had witnessed the disappearance of some 18,000 steam locomotives in just thirteen years from BR rails. One of these was First Great Western's Managing Director, Alison Forster, an old-school diehard who was still campaigning against steam as *Tornado* neared completion believing that her digital-era 'customers', as passengers were called for a sorry while in the early and crudest days of privatisation, wanted nothing to do with an essentially 19th Century technology. Running steam engines on the main line, she said, was like trying to land a biplane at Heathrow. But Forster was wrong. Unbeknown to such railway managers we were now living in an age of both/and rather than either/or technology; by 2010, we could own the latest computers and travel behind a brand new steam locomotive. And, why not? *Tornado* itself owes a great deal to computer technology.

In any case, not only are many of Britain's trains powered by steam (from power stations generating electricity through steam turbines), but many express trains running on today's Great Western are, by the standards of much of the rest of Europe, as old fashioned as a 'King' class 4-6-0 would have seemed to the likes of Alison Forster in the 1960s. The HST (class 43 trains, designed by BR at Derby and built at Crewe Works) that provide the mainstay of high speed services from Paddington to Penzance in 2010 are diesel-electrics, the youngest of which is now 28 years old and representative of an 'outdated' technology. These also happen, like 'Kings', 'Castles' and *Tornado* herself, to be fine, fast, well-designed and reliable machines popular with operators and the public alike.

It was also true, seemingly unbeknown to Alison Forster and the zealous anti-steam lobby, that many contemporary railway managers were secret steam enthusiasts. They might hide the fact in public and yet, without their support and encouragement, it would be all but impossible to operate the sheer level of steam specials run in 2010, much less to offer the steam expresses clear roads on main lines nominally reserved for 125mph passenger trains.

Even then, a new generation of enthusiasts and other travellers by rail was beginning to demand a far higher standard of service than old-school trainspotters had long been comfortable with. It was all very well to expect anyone with steam, Ian Allan *abc* locospotters books, Biros, Wagon Wheels, Ilford FP3 film and motorcycle engine oil in their blood to rise at some ungodly hour in the morning to ride all day in a run-down 1950s-era train at some painfully slow pace, and with terrible things to eat, and to arrive home in the cold and dark; but, an ever increasing number of people now used to good food, hotels and comfortable and stylish travel expected something better. This, is fact, is one of the key reasons *Tornado* exists: to run brisk and comfortable trains at godly hours, to make steam a pleasure to those would never really want to clamber through a grimy motive power depot in the winter, much less to stand and stare at the connecting rods of

a steam locomotive at a platform end for whatever ineffable purpose, nor to count rivets or write pedantic letters to the editors of enthusiasts' magazines.

The nature of those involved in the preservation and steam operating movement appeared to be changing, too. Although, perhaps, they had always been interested in railways and in the steam locomotive in particular, by 2000, lawyers, doctors, journalists, bankers, and many other professional people began to be unafraid to admit to the love that had not dared speak its name for many years: steam. Where, as Ian Jack, the steam-loving *Guardian* columnist and former editor of the literary review, *Granta*, and *The Independent on Sunday*, had once hidden his copy of *Steam Railway* behind *The Times Literary Supplement* or the *London Review of Books* on train journeys, now it was possible for him to be seen in full view of other passengers reading about the exploits of restored 'Jubilees' and 'Royal Scots'.

Today, there are some 2,000 steam locomotives at work in Britain. The standards set by miniature railways like the Romney Hythe & Dymchurch in Kent, by narrow gauge railways including the Ffestiniog and Welsh Highland in North Wales and by such regular main line operators as Steam Dreams [the 'Cathedrals Express'] and West Coast Railways [the 'Jacobite' and 'Scarborough Spa Express'] are high. And, *Tornado* aside, there are several steam locomotives currently under construction to fill in the gaps left by the hammer-blow of the 1955 Modernisation Plan.

One of the great inspirations for a new generation of steam builders was the story of BR '8P' No. 71000 *Duke of Gloucester*. The remains of this half-destroyed locomotive were still at Dai Woodham's Barry scrapyard in 1973 when the 71000 Preservation Society was formed. With help from big and small British businesses, a team of dedicated enthusiasts brought the locomotive back to life 13 years later. The result was not perfect, as, despite rectifying faults inherited from its original design and manufacture, the 71000 Duke of Gloucester Steam Locomotive Trust, as the society had become, knew full well that there was still much to do to develop the one and only purpose-built BR express passenger locomotive into the efficient modern engine she should have been when first built in 1954.

Even at this interim stage, *Duke of Gloucester* put up stirring performances, setting a number of records in the process (when had a steam engine with a heavyweight passenger train topped the fearsome Camden Bank up from the end of the platforms of London's Euston station at 41mph before?). Later on, and with a decent grant from the Heritage Lottery Fund, 'The Duke' was restored afresh at Crewe Works. Today, No. 71000 is a superb locomotive capable of performances that would have seemed improbable in the 1950s.

What the 71000 Duke of Gloucester Steam Locomotive Trust proved was that it was possible not just to restore a main line steam locomotive of such size and complexity, but to manufacture much of it from scratch. If the Trust could build the missing half of No. 71000, then why not a complete new locomotive? That, of course, is what the A1 Steam Locomotive Trust set out to do when it was formed in 1990. Clearly, steam had not come to an end in 1968; it was simply held at a signal waiting for the green light.

Overleaf: Although this shot of No. 60163 *Tornado* at Ropley on the Mid-Hants Railway was taken two decades after the formation of the A1 Steam Locomotive Trust, it is the dedication of the pioneers of preservation that paved the way for the magnificent achievement of its creation.
MATT HOWELL

CHAPTER FIVE

Dreaming Tornado

Great ideas are worth sharing

Tornado began as a dream. Or, more accurately, several overlapping dreams. David Champion, the A1 Steam Locomotive Trust's first Chairman, remembers reading an article in *Railway Modeller* magazine in the mid-1960s. A Northumbrian schoolboy at the time, Champion felt strongly that the author, who suggested the best way to remember steam in the future was to build models of extinct classes of locomotives, was wrong. A letter, that same year, from a W. K. Berry of Salisbury, in the November 1966 issue of *The Railway Magazine*, served only to strengthen Champion's resolve.

"As full-size locomotives require so much expensive storage space for their preservation", wrote Mr Berry, "I suggest that preservation societies consider the alternative of commissioning a large-scale model, say one inch to the foot. This would give an excellent impression, would require less storage space, and might even be cheaper than buying originals."

But, what about the sound, smell and sheer presence of a live, full-scale steam locomotive? A model, however intricately made and lovingly detailed, would never be able to capture these. The best way forward, Champion couldn't help thinking, was to build the real thing. The schoolboy harboured his dream. Years later – the early 1980s – Ian Storey, a locomotive engineer with his own workshop in Morpeth, was in Carnforth where he came across a spare boiler for the 'A3' No. 60041 *Salmon Trout*; this, he thought, might be the starting point for a new 'A1'. As chairman of the North Eastern

Build an A1

* All constituent parts for building an engine have been made individually as parts of restoration projects.

* Nobody has managed to do it yet for a main line loco – costs – this would be the largest single project ever carried out by steam movement. If it could be done by conventional railway preservation methods it would have been done by now.

* Therefore – such a large project needs 2 things –
  i) The best business organisation by professional businessmen
  ii) A funding system able to supply the unprecedented amounts of cash.

* Costs   About £1½m at todays prices – will rise with inflation

* Build Time   depends on money, but about 10 years probably.

* Funding System
  Needs to be   i) understood easily by everyone
                 ii) affordable by everyone.

If set up as charitable Trust – contributions grossed up 33%

Small, but regular contributions

£1.25 per week?

$1.25 \times 4 = £5 \times 12 = £60$ p.a., grossed up $= £80$ pa, £800 10 years

If keep level with inflation, say £1000 per contributor over 10 years.

$£1m ÷ £1000 = 1000$ people contributing.

Got to be 1000 people out there who will contribute £1.25 a week for a brand new A1 !!!

* High profile launch – professional

* Follow up with Roadshows round country.

The objectives scribbled on the wine-stained document penned by A1 Trust pioneer David Champion and his friends 20 years ago still hold firm today.
COURTESY OF DAVID CHAMPION

£1.25 = price of a pint

Slogan: "Build a brand new A1 for the price
of a pint of beer a week!!!"

1000 contributors should see it built
in 10 years.
Less and it takes longer
More and it is a quicker build.

This will work.

Locomotive Preservation Group and owner of No. 44767, an ex-LMS Stanier 'Black Five' 4-6-0 – a popular locomotive working specials on the main line – Storey knew pretty much exactly what might be involved in building a brand new steam locomotive.

In 1988, Mike Wilson, then working for ICI at its Billingham plant on Teesside, was campaigning to get Stockton Bank Top station listed. He came up with the idea of building a non-working replica of a steam locomotive associated with the station to capture the public imagination. For many decades, the Stockton & Darlington Railway's famous *Locomotion No. 1* had stood on the station's platforms. In 1975, this had been moved to the Darlington Railway Centre and Museum. What might replace it? Why not a replica of an 'A1'?

It was Mike Wilson who wrote to the now defunct *Steam Railway News* [April 1990] suggesting the idea of building a replica 'A1'. Champion, by now a director of the J. Rothschild Partnership, although a closet steam enthusiast, got in touch with Wilson. Champion explained that he had been waiting for someone to do just this – build an 'A1' – for years. Now, he realised, that if he could put the right team in place with the right balance of financial, engineering and business skills, it might just be possible to create a new Peppercorn Pacific. Through his work at Rothschild, Champion had met Ian Storey. From then on, the dreams of these men began to merge. Storey had the engineering skills, Wilson had supplied the idea, and Champion had the financial know-how. Equally importantly, he had well-connected contacts, many of whom proved, like him, to be secret steam enthusiasts. Steam was the love that dared not speak its name at the time; to be keen on steam was to be both wilfully old-fashioned and even a bit odd. A gricer. An anorak. A nutter. This might have been unkind and wrong, and yet there was no doubt that enthusiasm for steam carried the risk of being thought of as a badly-dressed and socially challenged number-cruncher standing on the end of lonely platforms, whatever the weather, with a Biro, notebook and camera specially designed for taking wholly uninteresting three-quarter-view snaps of trains that no-one, except fellow spotters, would ever remotely care to look at.

Champion knew he would also need a good lawyer. He found one in Stuart Palmer, a senior partner of Wallers Solicitors and a specialist in commercial law. Champion had approached Palmer after spotting him, camera in hand, at the North Yorkshire Moors Railway. "So, you're one of the faithful", he said; pleading guilty, Palmer joined Champion's dream team.

"We did sit around a dining table to discuss ideas", says Champion, "but one evening at home I drank a bottle of good red wine and wrote out the business plan that was – wine stains aside – the plan the A1 Trust stuck to. I've still got that piece of paper. It's like some holy relic of the back-to-steam movement."

Once word got out, other professional railway engineers and enthusiasts were quick to get in touch with Champion especially as the word spread through a newsletter (and later a very professional website – *www.A1steam.com*) edited by Champion's brother,

Phil, a schoolteacher. With one clear aim – "To build and operate a Peppercorn class 'A1' Pacific steam locomotive for main line and preserved railway use" – the nascent Trust was beginning to move away from the buffer stops.

"What was important from the beginning", explains Champion, "is that our message was simple and precise. We had no doubts about what we wanted to achieve. We're all North Eastern lads and we all shared a quiet passion for Peppercorn 'A1s', none of which was preserved."

In fact there was a representative of every class of important British Pacific on the preservation books by 1990 when the Trust came into being. Even the solitary BR Standard '8P' No. 71000 *Duke of Gloucester* had been saved, and rebuilt. In fact, the only Pacifics missing were the Great Western Railway's one and only *The Great Bear*, an experimental engine dating from 1908 that, in any case, had been converted into a Castle class 4–6–0 in 1924, the six original 'A2' Pacifics designed by Vincent Raven as rivals to Gresley's 'A1s' for the North Eastern Railway, the unloved BR Standard 'Clan' 4–6–2, the unpopular Thompson 4–6–2s that had preceded Peppercorn's 'A2s', and, of course, the 'A1s' that had followed on from their smaller wheeled siblings in 1948–49. Where these other missing Pacifics had rarely been mourned, by now the 'A1s' were much missed (although it has to be said that The Standard Steam Locomotive Company is currently building a new 'Clan' No. 72010, to be named *Hengist*). No-one, though, has yet announced plans for a new Thompson Pacific.

The upshot of that first meeting between Champion and the new A1 pioneers was the setting up of the A1 Locomotive Project on 17th November 1990, announced to a meeting of the Railway Institute, York, attended by more than 80 people including members of the press.

Several abiding principles were agreed and decisions taken. In the first place, the future 'A1' would not be a replica of a scrapped member of the class, but a brand new locomotive in its own right. This would be the 50th 'A1' numbered No. 60163, following on from the last of the original locomotives, No. 60162 *Saint Johnstoun*. "It is new locomotives like No. 60163", said David Champion at the time, "that will safeguard the future of nostalgic steam railtours and provide the motive power for the nation's preserved railways as existing locomotives become too delicate to be used on a regular basis."

Champion stressed that the new Pacific would not and could not be a carbon copy of the original 49 'A1s'. This was because since 1949 there had been many changes in regulations, materials and building techniques. Most of all, no private group outside the railways themselves had ever attempted to build a fully operating main line express passenger locomotive from scratch. Where locomotive works like Doncaster and Darlington had many decades of experience and know-how behind them, the A1 Locomotive Project would have to learn how to build No. 60163 without an established locomotive behind them and without anything like a Haynes Manual to show them how to do it. "There is a common misconception", said Champion, "that to build a locomotive you simply ask Andrew Dow, Head of the National Railway Museum [Dow held his post from 1992-94], nicely if you can copy his drawings, then the rest is a bit like putting an Airfix kit together at a 12in/ft scale. Nothing could be further from the truth."

What Champion promised backers of the project, and steam enthusiasts as a whole, was an 'A1' as true to the original as technically and legally possible. Because the Trust was made up of businessmen who happened to be steam enthusiasts, the project aims were clearly and realistically focussed from the beginning. The organisation of what Champion described as "the largest single project in railway preservation in Britain today" was based on four essential principles:

1. It would be run using the best business practices by people experienced in the appropriate areas.
2. The funding method would have to be simple, and capable of being understood and afforded by virtually anyone.
3. Because of the enormity of the task, there would have to be a single aim to focus on, the project's mission statement – "The building and operation of an 'A1' – against which all proposed actions would be judged.
4. The rules of the organisation would prohibit cliques and any form of elitism. Everyone would achieve recognition based on effort rather than size of chequebook. This would enable all efforts to go into the building of the 'A1'.

Presented in this matter of fact and business-like way, the project quickly gathered supporters, many of them professionals for whom such things mattered. "When I was a kid", says Champion, "about 40 per cent of schoolboys had a go at trainspotting; so, when we set up the Trust, I couldn't help thinking that, out there in the boardrooms of Britain, there must be some forty per cent of directors with at least a residual fondness for steam. If we approached them in a thoroughly business-like way and then played on their heartstrings, we might just be in with a chance."

Champion and Mark Allatt, the Trust's Marketing Director at the time, did a circuit of British boardrooms and did, indeed, return with donations and sponsorship. Many railway enthusiasts, latent or otherwise, who felt unable to reveal their steamy passion, opened up to Champion and Allatt. Now, at last, it was possible to be a serious professional person and a steam enthusiast. As for raising funds in a simple and popular way in the world outside boardrooms, the Trust came up with the slogan "An 'A1' for the Price of a Pint". It was hoped that enough supporters, or "covenantors", could be convinced to donate the price of just a pint a week (£1.50 at the time in North East England) and that this, multiplied many times would add up to the cost of building No. 60163. The planned cost was £1 million over a ten-year period. In fact, Champion believed it could be possible to complete the Pacific as early as 1998, or certainly by 27th September 2000 to coincide with the 175th anniversary of the opening of the Stockton & Darlington Railway. It was

Andrew Cook, Chairman of Sheffield-based William Cook Cast Products, has been enormously supportive of the *Tornado* project, including providing the driving wheels and the tender. With blackened face from a full-speed cab ride on the record-breaking run over Shap, he has also clearly enjoyed his outing on the completed engine.
MALCOLM CRAWLEY/A1 STEAM LOCOMOTIVE TRUST

to take the best part of another decade, and a further £2 million before No. 60163, now *Tornado*, turned a wheel under steam.

Realistically, the price of very many pints of IPA and other popular beers was never really going to pay for *Tornado* within a decade, or even two. Sponsorship, though, was readily forthcoming. British Steel met the majority of the cost of the specially rolled steel plate it supplied for the locomotive's frames. Steel needed for pins, bushes and shafts on the new engine were given by Macreadys, part of the steel and engineering division of Glynwed International, while William Cook Cast Products, the world's largest steel foundry group, produced *Tornado*'s 6ft 8in driving wheels on "very advantageous terms to the Trust."

A promise of £50,000 sponsorship from Allan Levy's publishing company, New Cavendish Books, meanwhile had come with a request that No. 60163 be named *Tornado* in view of the sacrifices being made during the first Gulf War by RAF crews flying Tornado jets. It was, without doubt, a fitting name: it sounded exactly right.

The team announced in summer 1993 was undoubtedly impressive. With Champion in the chair, the all-important Technical Director was David Elliott. A professional engineer, Elliott had begun his career in traction and rolling stock with BR before moving on to be become Contracts Manager for the aircraft manufacturer, Pilatus Britten-Norman. Mark Allatt, a professional PR manager and, at the time, Corporate Public Relations Manager with the Hoskyns Group, one of Britain's largest computer services companies, took on the role of Marketing Manager. Barry Wilson, a chartered accountant and Vice-President of the Bank of America Trust (Jersey) Ltd, was Director of Resources responsible for dealing with loans, sponsorship and benefits in kind. Ian Storey was Chief

Technical Advisor, advising the Trust on practical steam engineering. Birmingham Railway Museum's Chief Engineer, Bob Meanley, was Production Manager; Meanley's experience extended to the reconstruction of a replica London & North Western Railway Bloomer express passenger locomotive of the 1840s to supervising work on Corby Power Station. The Project Planner, and electronics expert, was Rob Morland, Electronics Director for the Generic Group and a volunteer driver and fireman on the preserved narrow gauge Talyllyn Railway on the west Wales coast.

Others on the team added extra professional weight. Together, the members of the Trust epitomised a new generation of steam enthusiasts; they were both managers working with up-to-the-minute businesses as well as steam buffs to the core. None had a problem balancing the demands of a computer-age world with the age of steam, nor, of course, with the enduring and elemental appeal of the steam railway locomotive itself.

"Along with the innovative fund raising", says Mark Allatt, "the targeted use of volunteers' professional skills seems to have been crucial for keeping the project afloat. One of our adages is 'you do for the Trust what you do for a living'. We didn't ever ask a bank manager to learn to weld. We asked him or her to look after the money."

The reaction to the plan was certainly positive. "The most professional thing I've seen in thirty years of railway preservation", said Julian Riddick, President of the A4 Locomotive Society. "A highly imaginative and ambitious project which will help to ensure the future of steam well into the 21st Century", declared Chris Leigh, Editor of *Steam World*." "So wonderfully British", offered Mike Satow, former Managing Director of ICA Teeside and builder of a replica of George Stephenson's *Locomotion No. 1* of 1825. "Arthur would have been delighted with what you're doing", added Dorothy Mather. Discussions held in 1992 with Sam Foster and Brian Penney of the BR Private Owner Locomotive Engineers, essential to ensure *Tornado* would be certified for mainline running, had also been wholly positive.

Significantly, the project also received generous, and accurate, coverage in the national press as well as in the engineering and steam enthusiasts' journals. From very early on, *Tornado* was something of a celebrity in the making. What also made the press prick up its ears was the fact that No. 60163 was to be built using the latest computer techniques in design and manufacturing. This made her different from the construction of small locomotives built since the end of steam on BR for miniature and narrow-gauge railways. *Tornado* was steam, but not old-fashioned steam.

The Trust had one further weapon up its sleeve. Of course such a word should never be linked to a lady like Dorothy Mather, and yet it was this charming, witty and wholly delightful woman who offered both a link to the personalities of the LNER's past and to a new generation who revelled in her company. "We couldn't be more delighted than to have someone so elegant and vibrant, going on nineteen", said David Champion when Dorothy, introduced by Geoff Drury who had known her for some years, agreed to become the Trust's President. "She knows about locomotives, and she knows steam.

A lady with unique memories of Arthur Peppercorn and life at Doncaster works in the days of steam. Dorothy Mather enjoys a tea after lighting the first fire in *Tornado's* firebox at Darlington Locomotive Works, 11th January 2008.
KATHLEEN ELTIS/A1 STEAM LOCOMOTIVE TRUST

She's a brilliant recruiter of new convenantors – she sees what we're doing from a slightly different angle, not quite so focussed on the pure engineering part."

Dorothy Mather was to help nurse *Tornado* into being just as she had looked after *Pepp* when it was announced that he was seriously ill a month after their wedding, celebrated at Doncaster, in September 1948. The only daughter of an LNER hydraulic engineer, who died in his 40s, Dorothy was brought up with the railway. As a young girl she had met Gresley, while the kind and courteous Peppercorn was a family friend. Pepp's shy, good manners extended to not collecting an OBE when he was awarded this honour (twice, in fact, it was later posted to him), and to finding it funny when engine crews had something to say about his locomotives. Dorothy Mather particularly likes the story of a day when Pepp, getting off a train hauled by one of his 'A1s', spoke to the crew, as he liked to do. The fireman told him, in no uncertain terms, "it's a good engine, sir, but I picked up the bloody shovel at King's Cross and didn't put it down again until Doncaster."

Dorothy took to her new role as President of the A1 Trust with aplomb, winning hearts and minds with her memories, wit, wide-brimmed hats and sheer sense of fun as well as duty. Her upbringing had been Doncaster, through and through, and yet Dorothy – who later married Colonel Bill Mather, one of the first British officers into the hell of Belsen in 1945 – brought charm, style, impeccable old world manners, an enviable dress sense and panache into a world of heavy engineering, sooty boiler suits, sweat and oily rags.

Originally, *Tornado* was to have been constructed at Doncaster. A partnership agreement was signed by the A1 Steam Locomotive Trust and Doncaster Metropolitan Borough Council, and a press conference held in July 1993 to celebrate the occasion. "Doncaster is a very special place for railway enthusiasts", said the Mayor of Doncaster, Councillor John Quinn, adding "it is where many great steam locomotives, including *Flying Scotsman* and *Mallard*, were built and maintained. This project will ensure Doncaster's position as a mecca for all those who are thrilled by the thoroughbreds of the world of steam."

Together with the council, the Trust promised a heritage complex at Doncaster; this was to be called the Gresley Centre, aimed at promoting long-term job creation, economic regeneration and tourism. "The Partnership Programme is a meeting of minds and hearts", said the Mayor. "Of minds, because the council is impressed with the business-like approach to this exciting and innovative concept – the building of completely new steam engines. Of hearts, because we feel strongly that the industrial heritage of this great railway town must be conserved."

Hearts and minds were not enough. The Doncaster connection fell through, as did the proposed Gresley Centre. There were several reasons why the Doncaster venture failed. At first, the Trust was offered space in the former GNR/LNER locomotive works, but as this was part of an open plan space, it was unsuitable for the Trust's needs; the team required its own dedicated area. After this, it was a former bus garage, which was not exactly the same thing as a locomotive works. But, it was also 'Donnygate' that encouraged

After plans to assemble new 'A1' Pacific No. 60163 *Tornado* at Doncaster came to nothing, enthusiastic support from Darlington Council ensured that public grants were made available for the historic Hopetown Works to be rehabilitated for its new purpose.
DAVID ELLIOTT/A1 STEAM LOCOMOTIVE TRUST

the Trust to think again about the South Yorkshire town. This was the unsavoury episode, played out from the mid-1990s, during which all too many of Doncaster's traditional Labour party elite proved to be corrupt – and had been for a number of years. By 1999, 27 local councillors had been arrested. It had been, said *The Guardian*, "the worst local government corruption case since the Poulson scandal of the 1970s."

This was a sorry state of affairs, and yet between the building of the Peppercorn 'A1s' and, later, BR 'Standard' locomotives in the 1950s, Doncaster had fallen on hard times. The picture painted by Nick Cohen in *The Guardian* in 1997, the year *Tornado*, or what existed of the locomotive at that time, moved to Darlington, was not exactly one that the Tate Gallery would want to hang on its walls: "Although it is pushing an image to describe Doncaster as Third World, the Yorkshire town is certainly all but surplus to the requirements of the 'free' market of the First. The pits are shut and Donny makes a living by supplying the most menial of services. Unskilled women work in call centres where time-and-motion men make sure they don't waste a second of company time. Unskilled men become warders in the de-unionised prison whose American owners have retained the right to profit from the deprivation of British citizens' liberty, even though five incarcerated customers found the service so slack they killed themselves last year [1998].

"Unsurprisingly, the young grab what pleasures they can and on a Saturday night the bars and their clientele are heaving. The local authority called for mass HIV testing after an outbreak of heterosexual AIDS among clubbers. In brief, Doncaster could do with a little help from its elected representatives."

For generations of railwaymen and enthusiasts, Doncaster had been an all but holy ground of steam engineering. The very name Doncaster spelt quality, as well as a famous racetrack and the beautiful express locomotives named after racehorses crafted in its world-famous Great Northern and LNER workshops. No-one in Peppercorn's day, much less Gresley's, could have predicted the decline and fall of this once proud town.

Although this was disappointing, Darlington, 75 miles north, proved to be a happy second choice. Given the fact that nearly half the original Peppercorn 'A1s' had been built here, the town made perfectly good sense. Here, too, was the perfect building in which to bring *Tornado* to life; this was the old Hopetown Carriage Works built in 1853 by Joseph Sparkes for the Stockton & Darlington Railway. So, here was a connection with George Stephenson, *Locomotion* and the first public railway to operate steam locomotives. Even better perhaps was the fact that Arthur Peppercorn had his office here from 1946.

As half the stone and slate building was to be used from 2001 as a workshop by the North Eastern Locomotive Preservation Works, it seemed only right that *Tornado* should take shape in this historic railway building where steam was alive and hissing again. The building was renovated with the help of European, national and local grants.

In an agreement with Darlington Borough Council, which owned the former Stockton & Darlington Railway Carriage Works, the A1 Steam Locomotive Trust was to set up its permanent base in what became known as Darlington Steam Locomotive Works early in 1996. The announcement was followed by a brief ceremony in front of *Locomotion No. 1*, the world's first public railway locomotive, now preserved in Darlington Railway Museum. At this ceremony, Councillor John Williams, Mayor of Darlington and Leader of Darlington Borough Council, presented the key to the new locomotive works to A1 Trust President Dorothy Mather.

"Ever since the original Darlington Locomotive Works was closed in 1966," said the Mayor, "there has been something missing from the town – the sight and sound of a new locomotive under construction. Although it is only eight weeks since the officers of Darlington Borough Council first met with the directors of The A1 Steam Locomotive Trust, in that time, we have seen a true meeting of minds.

"Darlington is a town with a great engineering past, yet it is successfully competing in the hi-tech world of the 1990s. This project, with its combination of traditional skills, first developed in Darlington nearly 175 years ago, and the latest computing and engineering technology, is an ideal symbol for our town."

Meanwhile, The Locomotive Construction Company – a wholly-owned subsidiary of the 'A1' Steam Locomotive Trust – had been set up to build *Tornado*. David Elliott had set the wheels in motion in 1993 by visiting the National Railway Museum [NRM] at York to see what drawings were available. These certainly existed – Indian ink tracings on linen – although they had never been catalogued or indexed. There was, however, no General Arrangement [GA] plan – a complete and detailed blueprint – for the 'A1'. As Elliott discovered, this had never existed, as the 'A1' was essentially an 'A2' with larger wheels, so the GA for the 'A2' had been used for the 6ft 8in locomotives. This had been no problem for engineers and skilled workers at Doncaster and Darlington in the late 1940s; they knew as if by instinct how to turn an 'A2' into an 'A1'.

Luckily, someone had been in to the NRM some while before gathering 'A1' plans for a five-inch gauge scale model. Over an exhausting three-day stint at the museum, Elliott and his team, including Gerard Hill and Bob Alderman, amassed four hundred primary and a further 400 secondary sheets of drawings. As LNER draftsmen had been encouraged to make maximum use of paper, several sheets included up to eight individual drawings of locomotive details. When added up, Elliott and Co had no fewer than 1,100 drawings or more than 90 per cent of a full set. This percentage crept up to 95 when a further 140 drawings were scanned in 2001. While this was good news, the problem was how to copy these large-format original drawings that had become frail over the years. The answer was digital scanning. One of Tornado's backers, Ray Pettit, a CAD [computer aided design] business manager, borrowed an A0 large-format scanner from Expert Graphics of Hanley Swan, Worcestershire. This mighty machine was shipped to York once an agreement had been hammered out between the A1 Trust and the NRM.

When Elliott began to pore over the digitised drawings on screen, it soon became apparent that there was not always enough immediate detailed information for these to be readily used in the design of *Tornado*. Not only were many of the drawings smudged or dirty, demanding a considerable amount of painstaking redrafting, but quite a number were labelled with such vague, and rather funny, expressions as "this bolt must be a good fit" or "Note: this item to be made with special care". Workmen of the 1940s, however, had known perfectly well how to make things – bolts, screws, seams, joints – that fitted a new locomotive without having to be given exact design specifications or even precise details of what material such components should be made of. Britain was a nation of producers at the time, not consumers as it is today; the country was skilled, lean and intelligent. In any case, it had just emerged from the most devastating war ever known; people, then, had got on with jobs requiring thought and experience as British industrial and engineering production reached an all-time high.

Having studied the drawings and considered how an original 'A1' might be built, Elliott quickly came to the conclusion that certain components would have to different from the way they had been designed and built more than half a century ago. The major difference was to be in the design and construction of the boiler. "The capacity to rivet a structure the size of an 'A1' boiler", wrote Elliott in the July 1993 issue of *The Railway Magazine*, "no longer exists – partly because modern health and safety legislation would make it difficult to have a person working inside a boiler while riveting." As a result, Bob Meanley was asked to design an all-welded boiler with a steel firebox rather than a riveted boiler with a copper firebox.

Other notable changes included a provision in the firebox for easy conversion to oil firing or a gas-producer combustion system, "against a time when good steam coal is no

longer available", the fitting of air brakes alongside traditional vacuum brakes [air brakes are faster and more powerful; all modern trains on the British mainline are air-braked], improvements to make controls on the footplate easier to use, and, all importantly, a subtle lowering of the engine's height so that *Tornado* would be able to run unimpeded under the overhead wires of electrified main lines.

One big question was the extent to which *Tornado* should be brought up to date in terms of thermal efficiency. The Trust's view, and certainly Elliott's, was that No. 60163 should be the 50th production 'A1' and not a highly modernised steam locomotive in the guise of a Peppercorn 'A1'. Of course it would be possible to tune the original design to give Tornado more power and greater efficiency as much had been learned in the area of thermo-dynamics since Peppercorn's spell as CME of the LNER. In the world of classic car restoration, an increasing number of owners want a sports or sporting car of the 1950s or '60s brought up to date with vastly improved brakes, handling, speed and power. In fact, at much the same time as the A1 Trust was set up, classic car companies like Vicarage Cars were being established.

Based at Bridgnorth, and close to the preserved Severn Valley Railway, Vicarage offered Mk2 Jaguars, at a cost, better than new. Although the company was careful not to modernise the cars in ways that would spell a loss of character, other outfits got in on the act and, soon enough, it was possible to buy a Mk2 Jaguar that might as well be a brand new car. The A1 Trust knew instinctively where and when to say no to modifications that would have transformed *Tornado* into a Mk2 'A1'.

Nevertheless, it was hard not to pay attention to a letter received in 1992 from Livio Dante Porta, the distinguished Argentinian steam locomotive engineer, a disciple of Andre Chapelon, and a man who had built some of the most efficient of all steam locomotives. Porta's letter was accompanied by a 200-page proposal on how the 'A1' design could be so improved that, when ready for the road, Tornado would be capable of running, quite comfortably, at up to 120mph and developing no less than 5,000ihp at 105mph.

In painstaking detail, Porta explained how a 'super-A1' might be produced. The aim was not just to develop great power and to run at mercurial speed, but to shape a locomotive that would have a better grip on the rails than the original 'A1s', cope with low quality coal, maintain high power over long distances with the least effort on the part of the crew – mechanical stoking was to replace hand-firing – and be welcome on Continental main lines. With new cylinders, a boiler pressed to 300psi and improvements made to the flow of steam through the locomotive, Porta had a vision of an 'A1' that would appeal to enthusiasts and yet be very much at home on the modern high-speed railway. This was certainly a consideration; one problem steam operators have suffered from in Britain to date is a speed restriction of 75mph on even the fastest of locomotives; given the fact that large-wheeled steam locomotives tend to accelerate far more slowly up to that speed than diesel or electric-powered trains, it was always going to be tricky to filter steam excursions through schedules created for modern trains. A true Super Pacific would remedy the situation.

David Elliott replied publicly to the Porta proposals in a letter to *Steam Railway* magazine published in October 2003. He pointed out that many of the innovations suggested by Porta had not been tried anywhere in Britain and that "nowhere in the world have they all been applied on a single locomotive." While this was no reason not to try, Porta himself had suggested that the 'A1+' would need at least 20,000 miles of testing to iron out any bugs. With tight finances, the Trust needed *Tornado* to come out of its box 100 per cent ready to work revenue-earning mainline trains with as little fettling as possible. It simply could not afford to act as some latter-day steam reseach and development outfit.

"All things considered", wrote Elliott, "we aim to adopt some – but not all – of Ing Porta's proposals, including a welded steel boiler and firebox, maybe increased superheat, streamlining of steam passages, redesigned valves, improved valve gear events and roller bearings. However, leading dimensions and the general layout of the locomotive will remain unchanged." Not wanting to sound too dry, Elliott added, "As a design point, we aim to take the Appleby-Ais Gill 'Blue Riband' conclusively! Given that the original 'A1' was similar in power to *Duchess of Hamilton*, *Duke of Gloucester* and *Blue Peter* with a theoretical disadvantage compared with the latter two engines over this route with 6ft 8in driving wheels, compared with 6ft 2in, we are looking for 10-15 per cent improvement to clinch it."

The formidable and lengthy climb up over the breathtaking Settle & Carlisle Line had long been a challenge to steam locomotive engineers; it demanded nothing less than a full head of steam over a considerable and challenging distance, and along tracks that were often wet and slippery. Porta could certainly have helped *Tornado* to an outright record, but common sense prevailed. The Trust could not afford to experiment with the fiftieth 'A1' and, in any case, its core message, declared by David Champion was "to build and operate a Peppercorn class 'A1' Pacific steam locomotive for main line and preserved railway use." A Peppercorn Pacific, that is, and not a locomotive that would have been beyond Pepp and his team's ken so very shortly after the Second World War. A Porta-Peppercorn 'A1' would, after all, have been a very different dream.

CHAPTER SIX

Building Tornado
It all goes to plan

No-one had built a large brand new standard gauge steam locomotive in Britain for more than 20 years. The final one, in 1971, had been one of the sturdy, and doggedly conventional 0-6-0 tank locomotive built by Hunslet of Leeds for industrial railway use. As for service on the main line, No. 92220 *Evening Star*, the last of 251 impressive BR Standard 9F 2-10-0s, took the dubious honours in March 1960 when she was rolled out from Swindon Works. Today, *Evening Star* is preserved – a national treasure at York and most recently at Swindon's STEAM museum – while a large proportion of the workshops where she was built have been turned into a 'designer retail outlet' shopping mall.

While there were many engineers, enthusiasts, preserved railways and even companies – like Hunslet – capable of restoring steam locomotives, making components for them and building small new engines for narrow-gauge and miniature lines, *Tornado* was, to say the least, something of a challenge when work began in earnest on creating the 160-ton Pacific in 1994.

Perhaps it was not surprising that there was talk – mostly rumour – of No. 60163 being built abroad. Main line steam was still at work in China, India, Poland and South Africa at the time and manufacturing skills had not yet been lost. The last broad gauge [5ft 6in] steam locomotive for the Indian Railways, one of a long line of 2,450 'WG' 2-8-2s had been manufactured at Chittaranjan Works in 1970; she was named *Antim Sitara* [Last Star], and ended her days, in 1996, working at a colliery. Production of narrow-gauge [metre gauge] locomotives continued for the next two years; the very last was a 'YG' 2-8-2. In South Africa, where many powerful British and German-built class '25NC' 4-8-4s held sway on the secondary main line from Bethlehem to Bloemfontein through the 1980s, it seemed as if steam was still very much in full swing. And it had been only in 1981 that the British engineer, David Wardale, had converted one of these muscular engines into a remarkably powerful and efficient modern steam locomotive, No. 3450 *L. D. Porta*, popularly known as the Red Devil.

In China, the last of no fewer than 4,700 'QJ' class 2-10-2s was built at Datong in 1988. There was something truly special – even slightly surreal – in watching a pair of these gigantic new locomotives pounding up and down the mountain passes of the brand new Jitong railway running between Tongliao and Jining in Inner Mongolia; opened in the mid-1990s, this new railway was worked entirely by steam in its first years. Except on special runs for foreign enthusiasts, the 'QJs', some little more than ten years old, were retired from this last great outpost of modern steam at the end of 2005. Again, dull diesels took over, and the British and American photographers went home.

Once it became easy to make visits, thanks to the efforts of worldwide tour operators such as British-based Tim Littler, this activity was a great spur for projects like the 'A1'

Right: The steam age looks set to finish where it began – in industry. In November 2009 a modern 'SY' 2-8-2, No. 1684, gently moves through a steelworks in China while cauldron wagons are filled with molten metal on the right.
TONY STREETER

Below: Sunset of steam? It may have disappeared from Britain's main lines in the 1960s, but if you search the remotest corners of the globe you can still find the invention that drove the industrial revolution hard at work. China is one of the last outposts, but even here steam is disappearing fast. On a freezing 18th November 2009 a little industrial 0-8-0 steams out of the sunset on the Huanan colliery railway in northeastern China.
TONY STREETER

Above: It is now almost 45 years since 'A1s' pounded the East Coast Main Line and daily steam now survives in only relatively few places – one of which is the romantic Harz mountain area of eastern Germany. One of the distinctive 1950s-built Harz engines roars uphill through the forests with a train from Wernigerode on an icy 30th December 2008.
TONY STREETER

Right: Other than Britain, Germany is probably the 'steamiest' country in Europe. On 14th February 2009 powerful 'Mikado' No. 41.1144 storms away from the historic town of Eisenach with a train that runs regularly during the winter sport season. *Tornado*'s boiler was built just 35 miles or so south of here, at Meiningen – the same place that this engine was rebuilt.
TONY STREETER

new-build, because it glorified the age of real main line steam to a new, young audience. Instead of listening to the fireside accounts from ageing railway supporters who belonged to an earlier generation and were not necessarily articulate, or indeed accurate, the opening up of easy access to the inner depths of China brought main line steam back to life. And while preserved lines of course have their benefits, there is nothing like seeing the real thing. The crews of the 'QJs' were certainly co-operative, affectionate and always smiling and nodding as a way of overcoming the language barrier. Selling a numberplate or a cap to a westerner with a loose wallet could double a driver or fireman's weekly wage – they allowed you to stoke the fire (for a small fee), surrender their cap and badge (for a another small consideration of course), even offering to give you the shovel they were using if you paid them a little more. At Datong depot, where the engines were still lined up in large numbers for their next rosters, relic sellers on scooters would try to get you to part with 500 US dollars for a brass cabside plate, reducing it to just 20 dollars as you boarded the coach or your primitively-equipped Inner Mongolian hotel, probably the last Western face they'd see perhaps for months.

It may have been on the other side of the world, yet Datong depot in midwinter honestly had the same crisp if acrid atmosphere of King's Cross, New England or Gateshead shed of the early 1960s. With their big smoke deflectors and high running plates, the appearance of the 'QJs' was not a million miles from an East Coast Pacific or British Railways '9F' 2-10-0, although their immense haulage power and pyrotechnic displays certainly were.

Closer to home, both PKP, the Polish State Railway, which, thanks to the involvement of British enthusiasts Howard and Trevor Jones, continues to run steam on regular commuter services between Poznan and Wolzstyn in 2010, and Germany, particularly the former East Germany, have remained havens of steam.

With its own steam locomotive plant at Meiningen, Deutsche Bahn (the German State Railway) was clearly able to build, if it cared to, as well as maintain steam locomotives in the 1990s. The A1 Trust, though, wanted *Tornado* to be built as far as technically possible in Britain. What was certain, given the dispersed state of steam know-how and manufacturing in Britain, was that *Tornado* would be built in many places, although assembled in Darlington. What also became apparent, and despite tendering at home, was that the boiler – the heart of the locomotive and the source of her great power would have to be sourced abroad.

But it all had to start somewhere. All that had existed of *Tornado* in the first four years of the Trust's existence were the frames for the locomotive's tender. These had been salvaged from the spare, eight-wheeled water-carrying tender converted to Alan Pegler's specifications for *Flying Scotsman* before she made her non-stop run from King's Cross to Edinburgh in May 1968. With the rusting water tank removed, the tender's frames were grit-blasted back to bare metal before being fitted with roller-bearing axleboxes.

The real birth of a new locomotive is regarded as the assembly of the main frames, and the workshops of the Birmingham Railway Museum at Tyseley is where *Tornado*'s frames were created. The date is 25th May 1996.
TED PARKER/A1 STEAM LOCOMOTIVE TRUST

Choosing a name for the new 'A1' was one of the earliest, easiest and most pleasant tasks for the Trust, although on 25th May 1996 there wasn't very much else to put on display apart from the cast plate and the undercoated main frames. President Dorothy Mather was nevertheless impressed with the elaborate crest honouring the Tri-National Tornado Training Establishment.
ROB MORLAND/A1 STEAM LOCOMOTIVE TRUST

Power to their elbows. *Tornado* is powered by three cylinders, one of which is placed inside the frames. A1 Trust Chairman David Champion and President Dorothy Mather inspect the heavy casting outside Tyseley Locomotive Works in 1996.
ROB MORLAND/A1 STEAM LOCOMOTIVE TRUST

The first parts of No. 60163 itself to take shape were her 48ft 6in frames. The steel for these was rolled at British Steel, Scunthorpe in 1994 and cut, from a single sheet, at a specialist branch of British Steel at Leeds; the button to set the cutting machine in motion was ceremoniously pushed by Dorothy Mather. The frames were then machined by T M Engineers of Kingswinford in the West Midlands and dispatched to the Birmingham Railway Museum – also known as Tyseley Locomotive Works – where they were assembled the following year. These were meant to have been assembled at Doncaster, but by this time, the negotiations with the local council had broken down. They were also, according to the Trust's Technical Director David Elliott, "probably the most accurate steam locomotive frames ever produced."

As *Tornado's* frames were under construction, so patterns for her three cylinders were ordered from Kings Heath Patterns, Birmingham. Even by the end of 1994, with so little to see of the complete locomotive, it was clear that the construction of *Tornado* was to be a collective effort made by numerous firms up and down the country. When the first 49 'A1s' were built the locomotive workshops of the leading railways were able to make just about every last component themselves. Specialist parts, whether footplate gauges or speedometers, might have been sourced outside the works, yet there was nothing like the scramble for major parts necessary to shape *Tornado*.

The following year the nameplates arrived, handed over by the RAF in a ceremony held at Birmingham Railway Museum. The cylinders, weighing three tons apiece, were cast, while patterns of the 6ft 8in driving wheels were supplied by William Cook Cast Products of Sheffield. The wheels themselves arrived at Tyseley from Lloyds of Burton-upon-Trent in 1996. Meanwhile, negotiations proceeded apace with Darlington Borough Council who proved willing to let the historic locomotive works building at an appropriate Peppercorn rent. While Hopetown Carriage Works was being restored during 1997, *Tornado's* cylinders and cab were bolted to the newly completed frames after these had been put on temporary display at the National Railway Museum, York. This was to show that *Tornado* now officially existed and, of course, to eke out more, much-needed publicity if the goodwill that had started the construction process was going to stretch for what was clearly several years into the future – and certainly well beyond the original optimistic deadline.

Meanwhile, British Timken donated not just the roller bearings the locomotive needed, but the expertise to fit and test them, too. Paul Ambler set up a website for the Trust, while grants totalling £300,000 were made by the EU, Darlington Borough Council and the National Heritage Memorial Fund. Some years earlier, David Champion had tried to enlist support from the Heritage Lottery Fund; his employer at the time, Jacob Rothschild, was Chairman of the Fund. Champion approached him at a dinner at the Dorchester Hotel, Park Lane, one evening. Rothschild thought *Tornado* a splendid idea, but had to disappoint Champion: because it was a new-build project, *Tornado* could not be considered 'heritage'. Future heritage? Perhaps, but the HLF's remit did not allow it to indulge in semantics. Funding would have to come from elsewhere. This, though, has remained an interesting issue for projects like *Tornado*, for, in a sense, this has been a heritage project; certainly few would disagree today that *Tornado* is a part of our collective or national heritage. Still, this status should help her with funding in years to come, and there seems to be no reason why the newest 'A1' will not be in steam for the next 50 years and more.

Throughout the prolonged process of construction, the Trust dreamt up any number of events to maintain public interest and support, and belief, among those covenanters who were paying money every month into *Tornado's* kitty. A lively A1 Trust convention was held every two years; the fourth of these, in September 1997, marked the formal opening of Darlington Locomotive Works, complete with smoke and a patriotic blast of Elgar's *Pomp and Circumstance March No. 1* [best known as Land of Hope and Glory] pounding through the early Victorian building.

However, the question of who would make the boiler threw a spanner in the all-British works. Discussions, the following year, with the Whessoe Technology Centre, Darlington, hit the buffers; it would have been convenient if the boiler had been made locally; but, the fact that twelve British companies were approached and only three bothered to reply was either a case of bad manners, or a sign of the technological times. It looked as if a boiler as big as *Tornado's* was beyond British engineering know-how. Still, there was plenty of work to do before the boiler had to be ordered.

In 1999, the gigantic connecting rods were forged at Hesketh's foundry in Bury, Lancashire. This was as much an emotional as a manufacturing process; it was extraordinary for Trust members to witness these great steel components being made in much the same way as they had been half a century earlier. The forgings for *Tornado's* three, 7ft 6in connecting rods were formed from cast steel billets each measuring a foot square and weighing five tons. They were shaped by immensely skilled workers using a one-ton hammer whilst heated to between 860 and 1200 degrees Centigrade. Each of the fully machined rods was to weigh just 22cwt [1.1 tons]. The poet, William Blake, spoke of the factories of the Industrial Revolution in terms of 'dark, satanic mills'; here, though was the brightest mill imaginable, with flames and sparks shooting from rods of glowing molten steel. It was a deeply impressive, if slightly terrifying sight. A reminder, too, of just how noisy and sensational steam locomotive engineering works must have been in full swing, whether in Doncaster, Darlington or Datong. Hesketh's has since closed.

What was becoming increasingly clear was that No. 60163 would be a product of both venerable and ultra-modern technology and methods of production. A culture of mugs of tea and packets of biscuits perched on the frames as *Tornado* took shape was matched, later in 1999, by Rolls-Royce, manufacturers of the RB199 jet that powered the RAF's Tornado jets, becoming a sponsor. The celebrated aerospace company agreed to machine the parts of *Tornado's* motion – the complete set of parts connecting the locomotive's pistons, cylinders, reversing gear and coupling rods to its 6ft 8in driving wheels – at its works at Hebburn, the Northumberland town's largest employer.

Meanwhile, Ian Howitt, a *Tornado* convenantor, had made the smokebox door at Crofton, Yorkshire; now *Tornado* had a face, especially once its BR-style numberplate was fixed to the upper door hinge. At much the same time, a decision was made to sell the 70-year-old tender frames the Trust had bought earlier to Flying Scotsman Services; these would become the chassis for a new second tender for the 'A4' Pacific No. 60019 *Bittern*. William Cook cast the wheels for *Tornado's* leading bogie, driving wheels and trailing pony truck and these were sent to Riley & Son at the East Lancashire Railway, Bury, to be fitted with new steel tyres. The structure of the cab was completed at Darlington, with David Champion and Mark Allatt the first people to sit inside on temporary seats; the production bucket seats were made by Marshalls of Cambridge, the aircraft outfitters, three years later.

The cab, which while relatively simple to construct, was seen as a milestone in the *Tornado* project. A decade before it was used on the railway, A1 Trust Chairman David Champion and Tyseley Chief Engineer Bob Meanley pretended to be train crew on 27th September 1997.
ROB MORLAND/A1 STEAM LOCOMOTIVE TRUST

Right: The axleboxes holding the wheels slide up and down to give some sprung suspension, against thickened plates attached to the frame called hornblocks. Barry Wilson and Ian Howitt use an air drill to ream a bolt hole for a hornblock liner fixing on 12th July 2002.
BARRY WILSON/A1 STEAM LOCOMOTIVE TRUST

Second right: The acceptable face of *Tornado*. The new steam-tight smokebox door, primed in grey undercoat, is ready to be fitted to the smokebox on 25th November 2000.
ROB MORLAND/A1 STEAM LOCOMOTIVE TRUST

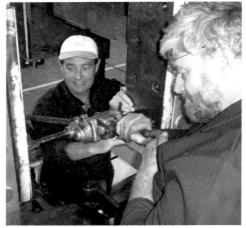

Looking forward along from the cab along the length of the frames, Allatt and Champion could now see the smokebox and chimney – cast by Charles W. Taylor at the North Eastern Foundry, South Shields – and all twelve wheels below them, but there was still a gaping hole where the boiler needed to be. A banner hanging where the boiler would one day be, appealed for £250,000 to fill the gap. One convenantor, Bruce Robinson, began collecting aluminium cans to help meet the cost; he sold these to Albert Draper, the very firm that had scrapped the last Peppercorn 'A1' No. 60145 *Saint Mungo* in 1966.

In 2000, with a plethora of projects being announced for the construction other new British mainline steam locomotives, including a Great Western Railway Churchward four-cylinder 'Saint' class 4-6-0, David Elliott joined the team full-time as Chief Engineer, while David Champion handed on the chairmanship of the Trust to Mark Allatt, the Trust's first Marketing Director and a hugely effective PR man and fund-raiser.

The fact that Allatt is 6ft 8inches tall – the exact same height as *Tornado's* driving wheels – made him, perhaps, the ideal man to take over in the driving seat of No. 60163. Allatt is a marketing professional, a former Head of Corporate Communications for Cap Gemini UK, Head of Marketing for KPMG Consulting, Marketing Director for GVA Grimley and Global Brand Director for Deloitte. Today, he is Marketing & Business Development Director for Shepherd & Wedderburn, the leading British law firm. He is also one of the founders and General Secretary of Conservative Way Forward, a Thatcherite pressure group. Typically, he chose to fight the Labour stronghold of Jarrow in the 1997 General Election. He lost.

Allatt was born in 1965, "too young", he says, "to remember an 'A1' in a scrapyard, let alone in action." There is a photograph of the five-year-old Allatt, however, taken at an open day at Barrow Hill shed in 1970, admiring 'A2' No. 60532 *Blue Peter*. This was to be the start of a lifelong obsession with LNER Pacifics. By the end of his first year in the chair, and as Britain moved properly into the 21st Century, *Tornado* was half-complete.

With other components arriving from across the Midlands and the North of England, 2001 looked to be a good year, but the re-organisation of the Hopetown Carriage Works to make room for the North East Locomotive Preservation Group and with a number of "non-conformances" to sort out – parts of the frames that failed to meet the latest regulations that would allow *Tornado* to run on the mainline – slowed the project. With the arrival of the NELPG, the Trust's workshop was reduced to a space measuring less than 100ft long by 50ft wide. As an 'A1', with its tender, is approximately 73ft long, Tornado finally emerged as if from a matchbox, and as if it was an '00' scale model rather than the real, superheated thing.

Actually, the year had gone rather badly, as Mark Allatt is the first to admit. For some ineffable reason, and out of the blue, one of the convenantors made allegations that the Trust was "in danger". Why? Because there was something wrong with the frames. If this was left unsorted, then *Tornado* would be unsafe. The Trust had to be rescued. This was odd given that the Trust was in safe hands. Nevertheless, it was decided to test the allegations. An outside agency was paid a five-figure sum to conduct tests. These showed that there were indeed 59 'non-conformances' that needed rectification, although a 'non-conformance' is not the same thing as a defect. These cost a total of £13,908 to put right, although the cost was met largely through manufacturers' warranties.

Three months later, further allegations were made that all was not well. Allatt held convenantors meetings to address the problem, and the Trust was soon back on an even keel. Not soon enough, though. Time spent in addressing allegations, meetings and a slow down on construction had meant a loss, calculated by the Trust, of £150,000 in wasted management time and a further £31,500 in lost income. Fortunately, only a handful of convenantors opted out, fearing, perhaps, that something had gone very wrong. It hadn't, yet Allatt calls 2001 the Trust's "annus horribilis".

"All organisations over a certain size tend to become a bit political", says Allatt, "and, yet, despite this one hiccup, we've worked closely and remarkably happily together. The worst thing is the time we wasted faffing about slowed the project down by something like 18 months to two years."

One very big decision, however, was all but resolved that year: it looked as if the contract for the all-welded steel boiler and firebox would be awarded to DB's Dampflokwerk Meiningen in Germany. In the event, it was another three years before the work began. During that time, negotiations had continued with rival boiler makers, but it was Meiningen's quietly concealed enthusiasm, as much as its ability to work comfortably with demanding EU regulations, that won the day. Before the contract was signed – in January 2005 – the A1 Trust launched a £500,000 bond issue to finance the cost of the new boiler.

It late 2001, the author of this book got in touch with the A1 Trust for the first time, travelling up to Darlington from London to make sense of what Tornado was and what exactly was happening in the old Hopetown Carriage Works. The following article appeared in *The Guardian* on 24th November under the headline, "Remembrance of Things Fast"; it was an attempt to capture the spirit of the Trust at that time, and when there was still so much to do, and so much money and sponsorship still to raise:

This is the country that invented the steam locomotive and the public railway. The first locomotive was built by Richard Trevithick, a Cornish engineer, in 1804. The first public railway, the Stockton & Darlington, opened 21 years later. A little more than 175 years on, my deep-blue 125mph GNER train pulls into Darlington Bank Top station no more than 20 minutes late. I'm here to see *Tornado* taking shape in the nearby Hopetown Carriage Works.

Tornado is the only main line railway locomotive under construction in Britain. Where are the *Locomotions*, the 'Stirling Singles', the *Flying Scotsmans*, the *Mallards* and the *Crepellos* of yesterday? Those that do still crop up run in China, Italy, the Czech Republic; anywhere except the land of Trevithick and the Stephensons. By common consent,

Britain's railways have lost the plot since privatisation. The network, and the GNER in particular, is still reeling from the accident last 17th October, when the 12.10 Leeds express, travelling at 115mph, went off the rails near Hatfield in Hertfordshire, killing four passengers and injuring many others. Railtrack was given a fresh £1.5 billion public subsidy soon afterwards to put its house in order, but now the government has removed the props. The House of Railtrack has collapsed.

The debate now is whether or not the government will take the railways back into public ownership. At the moment, this seems improbable. Whatever happens, the nationalised British Railways that built *Tornado's* predecessors at the end of the 1940s is unlikely to steam back into business.

But even if we wanted them to be, the railways today could never revert to what they were half a century ago: too much steam and diesel smoke has passed under the bridge since then.

The engineering works at Darlington, and at Doncaster, 74 miles to the south, have long since lost the status and the skilled workforces that once placed them among the wonders of the railway age. It seems an eternity ago that Ian Allan Locospotters' Club specials – packed to their varnished-teak gunwales with enthusiastic boys of all ages (and a few recalcitrant sisters) – would steam up from King's Cross to take down the numbers and count the rivets of the steam racehorses stabled at Doncaster, Gateshead, York and Darlington.

Of course there were no Nintendos then, few private cars, and very little spare cash. Nor did boys, heads chock-full of batting averages and the technical specifications of aircraft and engines, go shopping, except to gawp at the Hornby-Dublo, Triang and Märklin model locomotives they dreamed of for Christmas. Hornby-Dublo happens to have done well recently, but it is adults, nostalgic for the days of steam and integrated railway systems, who buy their train sets.

"Certainly until the end of regular steam in 1968, our railways, although a little ragged around the edges, were something to enjoy and feel a part of. Engineers were giants and enginemen working-class heroes. Bill Hoole, one of the best known East Coast Main Line drivers, was the subject of an Ian Allan biography on sale in high street bookshops. When he retired, Hoole went to work as a driver on the narrow-gauge Ffestiniog Railway in North Wales. He signed his letters 'Driver Hoole', as enginemen did. In Hoole's day it was not unheard of for SNCF ingénieurs (engine driving was considered more a science than a job in France) to time their holidays so that they could accompany their locomotives as they went through their annual overhaul. It's hard to imagine the drivers of, say, Virgin or Connex getting quite so excited by their engines at the beginning of the 21st century, much less anyone writing up their life stories.

Locomotives and railways stirred passions. They still do, of course, but the emotions today tend to be negative ones. Artless, craftless and disturbingly bereft of engineering skills and management know-how, Britain's railways are no longer the fond joke they once were: they aren't remotely funny. No-one involved in their running, with the partial exception of GNER [Great North Eastern Railway, now disenfranchised], whose trains at least look like trains should, appears to give a damn. If only we could inject into this privatised mess some of the enthusiasm that used to inform and support the railways.

This is where *Tornado* plays her part. When I arrive at the former Hopetown Carriage Works, she appears to be in pieces: wheels here, cab there. There's her face – the smoke-box door – tucked in a corner. Her high-pressure welded steel boiler has yet to arrive. A tightening of thousands of imperial-measure bolts, *Tornado* is a reproduction of a 1948 'A1' Peppercorn Pacific, honed from the nation's finest materials and components. Labels of parts bear the legends Birmingham, Renishaw, Tyseley, Darlington, Bury, Cambridge, York, Scunthorpe, Doncaster, Teesside, Leeds. The high-pressure boiler, though, may yet have to come from abroad: with each passing month, Britain loses more and more of its heavy engineering business.

Tornado will pull luxury and other special trains at 100mph and more, its cab, crew, instruments and workings filmed by on-board cameras. These will relay images to passengers riding behind her under plumes of superheated steam. Railtrack normally limits steam locomotives to a 75mph canter, not quite fast enough to thrill; because *Tornado* will be brand-new and equipped with all the latest gadgetry to make it compatible with modern electrics and diesels, this 3,500-horsepower loco will be allowed to gallop.

The original 49 'A1s' (23 from Darlington, 26 from Doncaster) cost £16,000 apiece. That's about £330,000 today, which represents tremendous value; a similarly-powered diesel engine costs about 10 times that amount. However, because there is no steam locomotive works in contemporary Britain and thus no batch production to spread costs, the final bill for *Tornado* and the A1 Steam Locomotive Trust will be £1.7 million. To date, somewhere between 1,600 and 1,700 enthusiasts are paying for it by deed of covenant. All contributions are gratefully received.

Mark Allatt, a marketing director, is the Chairman of the A1 Steam Locomotive Trust. At 36, he's too young to have seen 'A1s' at work, much less heard the compelling, jazz-like rhythm of *Kestrel* or *Sea Eagle* harrying the 'Talisman' across the racing flats between York and Darlington. He never stood at the trackside as *Hal o' The Wynd* or *Saint Mungo* blasted the weighty umber-and-cream 'Yorkshire Pullman' up from King's Cross to Hatfield and the north, all starched white tablecloths, cut glass, pre-BSE beef, twin-sets and polished silver. The same height as Tornado's six driving wheels, Allatt is passionate about steam. He is also as far as could be from the stereotypical image of the railway enthusiast. A few weeks before our trip to Darlington, Allatt fought off three hefty muggers who failed to rob him of his laptop in south London. His hands are heavily bandaged. He has further knife wounds in his arm and back.

Andrew Dow – an outwardly bluff, ruddy-cheeked, very funny former Rolls-Royce aircraft sales manager – joins us at York. As well as being *Tornado's* Sponsorship Director,

he chairs and advises numerous steam and railway trusts and charities. Dow Senior was head of public relations for the London & North Eastern Railway and the author of a three-volume history of the Great Central, which was absorbed by the LNER.

David Elliott picks us up from the neo-Gothic spectacle of Bank Top station. Like Allatt and Dow, he's the sort of man you would want on your team whatever you were doing: hugely knowledgeable, he's a railway and aircraft engineer who is now employed full-time building *Tornado*.

Dorothy Mather is the A1 Trust's President. Immaculately turned out, she refers to hotels as "'otels". Alan Bennett would have loved her. She is the widow of Arthur Henry Peppercorn (1889-1951), the last chief mechanical engineer of the LNER, who supervised the design and construction of the 'A1' Pacifics. "I was with the Coal Commission during the war," she says. "I met Pepp there. He was 30 years older than me. A lovely man, kind and very funny. He was working under Thompson [Edward Thompson, LNER's chief mechanical engineer – CME – from 1941-46]. Do you know what Thompson said? If Pepp married me, he would never get the CME's job. Well…"

Tornado was willed into life in 1990 by a loose association of high-powered engineers, solicitors, City financiers and telecommunications experts, along with a print buyer, a master brewer, a designer and a history teacher. Successful professionals, men and women, with a genuine love of railways. Not a nutter or 'anorak' among them.

Doncaster Council was decidedly unhelpful when the *Tornado* team made an approached in 1993. It was going through 'Donnygate' at the time – a minor corruption scandal; but the *Tornado* project made no impact on this gerontocratic, Labour-run Yorkshire town as it moved from being a centre of mining and engineering excellence to a dreary shopping centre with a theme park attached. (At the Doncaster Leisure Park you are served popcorn by young men Velcroed into Casey Jones railroad engineer outfits. Their dads built railway locomotives at Doncaster works; their grandfathers steamed past on the footplates of Gresley, Thompson and Peppercorn Pacifics.)

Darlington Town Council was keener to help, although the old locomotive works had been supplanted by a branch of Morrisons. The councillors offered instead the Hopetown carriage works, built in 1853, for what Allatt says was a 'Peppercorn rent'. As the contract was signed, *Tornado*'s steel frames were being plasma-cut, guided by a computer – the high-tech side of the construction was already under way in Tyseley, south of Birmingham. Muck, brass and plasma.

"It was a lovely town, Doncaster, then," says Mather, who has driven up for lunch from Yarm, a South Yorkshire village. "Darlington, too."

Railway engineering at the time made the technology of the contemporary motor industry, yet to pose any sort of threat to the trains, look almost primitive – compare the speed and aesthetics of a boxy 1935 Austin 10, beetling up the A1 trunk road at a draughty 40mph, with the 'Silver Jubilee', cocktails, air-con and business deals pulsing past.

"Of course, the pre-war railways weren't perfect", says Dow. "There was never a golden age. The LNER was hard pressed financially, but there was a culture of making things, of public service within private enterprise, that is hard to understand today. The railways behaved, up to a point, like a well-oiled military machine."

In its first year of service, the 'Silver Jubilee', despite having to thread between plodding goods trains and grope through pea-soupers in the days before colour-light signals, was very nearly always on time. Not one of the four purpose-built 'A4' streamlined locomotives assigned to it suffered a mechanical failure. Clergymen's sons would not allow such sins.

The fiery energy of *Tornado* is created from the boiler barrel and firebox, which are being welded together at Meiningen in eastern Germany on 12th July 2006.

GRAHAM NICHOLAS/A1 STEAM LOCOMOTIVE TRUST

When it steams out in two years time, *Tornado* is likely to be the finest locomotive at work on Britain's atomised railways: an update of a machine designed just before the railways were nationalised. An echo of the glory days of British engineering, of working-class heroes, of achievements rather than accidents.

As we leave Darlington and thrum south with GNER, just matching the pace of Mallard down Stoke Bank, I'm wishing the A1 Steam Locomotive Trust could be given a commission to design and build a new generation of British railway locomotives, but they have already committed to their next project: a re-creation of the spectacular 1934 Gresley 'P2' 2-8-2 No. 2001 *Cock o' The North*, another machine – a highly impressive machine – from the past. Yet, if only the steam in the blood of Allatt, Dow, Elliott, Mather and company could be injected at high pressure into our wheezing, clanking railways, we might begin to learn to love them all over again.

The great symbolic achievement in 2002 was *Tornado's* moving for the very first time; not in steam, of course, but by now the Trust had a rolling chassis on its books. One of the key questions raised the following year was how *Tornado* would be fuelled. Oil and coal were the obvious contenders and, initially, oil was chosen. Modern oils would burn cleanly and efficiently; they would also mean no cinders, a potentially cleaner exhaust and, given the unreliable quality of modern coal – especially now that the mines that had once been so important a part of the economies of towns like Doncaster were long closed, if not exhausted – it seemed a more reliable option from a thermal as well as supply point of view. In 2004, however, the Trust decided to revert to coal. The price and future supply of oil had become as uncertain as events in the Middle East.

Graeme Bunker [Operations Director] and Graham Nicholas [Quality and Certification Director] joined the board in 2004. Bunker was Managing Director of Arriva Trains Wales at the time, and would later become Managing Director of Steam Dreams, the successful railway charter company that employs *Tornado* along with other first-rate British express passenger steam locomotives. Nicholas is a railway engineer; he would do much to ensure that *Tornado* was certified for main line running. To support Bunker's role – looking after *Tornado* out on the main line in the years to come – the Trust bought a support coach, acting on a tip-off from long-time enthusiast, fellow journalist, businessman and loyal Trust supporter Howard Johnston. This marked the end of a long search, and the vehicle in question was a BR Mk 1 Brake First Composite, No 21249. Built at Swindon in 1961, it was stored by the Great Central Railway at Ruddington before being transferred to Darlington in October 2008. Restored at a cost of £50,000 and running in 2010, this was to be Bunker's command centre, or bunker, once *Tornado* was fully certified and in passenger service. Loaded with spare parts, laptops, fitters, helpers, a lavatory and washroom, a kitchen, sleeping berths – "the snorers separated from the non-snorers", says Bunker – and tea, tea and more tea, coaches like these, coupled behind steam locomotives, help immeasurably with their smooth running.

During 2005, the boiler finally began to take shape at Meiningen, a place of pilgrimage for steam enthusiasts especially since 1990 when the former East German Deutsche Reichsbahn works, now in the hands of the new, pan-German DB, was made over to the repair and maintenance of preserved locomotives. The handsome buildings of what was now known as Dampflockwerk Meiningen, had been built in 1910 for the Prussian State Railway, replacing an earlier works opened in 1863. By a stroke of good fortune, the works, deep in the heart of Thuringia, survived Allied air raids and other military action. Taken over by the US Army in spring 1945, the works was soon back in action. Naturally, it was kept very busy indeed in the years immediately following the Second World War.

Aside from maintaining locomotives, the works also carried out such fascinating commissions as the transformation, in 1961, of the high-speed, pre-war streamlined tank locomotive No. 61 002 into the elegant Pacific 18 201. Designed for use in high-speed trials, No. 18 201 is still in action – restored at Meinigen in 2002 – and, with an official speed limit of 180km/h (112mph), a pace it can easily reach, this handsome green Pacific is the fastest steam locomotive operating anywhere in the world today. An 'A1' has only

Chief Engineer David Elliott has never been frightened from getting his hands dirty. Here he is in the inspection pit on 5th October 2002.
ROB MORLAND/A1 STEAM LOCOMOTIVE TRUST

Left: We're England-bound. It's 12th July 2006, and the newly-constructed boiler and firebox are ready to leave Meiningen in Germany for Darlington, where they will be installed in *Tornado's* frames.
DAVID ELLIOTT/A1 STEAM LOCOMOTIVE TRUST

Below: The boiler is carefully positioned above the frames prior to installation at Darlington Locomotive Works on 28th June 2007.
DAVID ELLIOTT/A1 STEAM LOCOMOTIVE TRUST

ever been recorded at a maximum of 102mph; it would be interesting to discover if *Tornado*, with her Meiningen boiler could, one day, give No. 18 201 a run for her money.

While Meiningen pressed ahead with the boiler, David Elliott and his team were up to all sorts of tricks to complete *Tornado's* chassis. Brake controls and sanding equipment were recycled from two withdrawn ex-BR Class 86 3,500hp electric locomotives stored at Shoeburyness. It was intriguing to see parts of electric locomotives introduced at much the same time as the last 'A1s' turned their wheels under steam on BR being used in the recreation of the technology they had once superceded. A mechanical lubricator, meanwhile, was received in Darlington from South Coast Steam Ltd; it had formerly been a part of an ex-MOD diesel shunter. So, by now it might be said that *Tornado* had both a little diesel and electric DNA in her blood. In this, as with the fitting of an 'A4' chime whistle, *Tornado* was certainly different from her older, austerity-era siblings.

The accuracy with which she was built also set *Tornado* apart from the earlier 'A1s'. According to David Elliott, the wheels, for example, were so smooth that the complete locomotive could easily be pushed out of the works by human power alone, while, if it was lifted above the rails, the entire wheel and motion arrangement could be turned by hand. A computer simulation had been used to assist in the setting up of the valves and motion, while the fine materials used and the cutting and aligning of the frames and motion to exacting modern tolerances all helped in the making of what would prove to be a very free running, and well-made, locomotive. *Tornado*, of course, had the advantage over the first generation of 'A1s' in being built as slowly and as methodically as they had been all but rushed out from Darlington and Doncaster in 1948-49.

In 2007, *Tornado's* driving wheels were spun – with the help of electric motors – at very high speed at Dowding & Mills, Birmingham, to balance the weights now fitted to

Opposite: A1 Trust Vice-President and Gresley Society Chairman Malcolm Crawley worked with the great steam designers, so it was appropriate for him to shovel the first coal into *Tornado*'s firebox at the first steaming of the boiler on 9th January 2008.
DANNY HOPKINS/STEAM RAILWAY

Left: It was a privilege for all present to witness Arthur Peppercorn's widow Dorothy Mather throw the lighted rags into *Tornado*'s firebox, ending the 32-year absence of an 'A1' Pacific in steam.
DANNY HOPKINS/STEAM RAILWAY

counteract the thrust of the newly complete motion. The tender was completed at North View Engineering, Darlington, and a huge number of works were carried out during the year concerned with the locomotive's brakes, injectors, superheater, pipework and fittings. And now the 21-ton boiler and firebox, delivered by sea, road and crane to the Darlington works in July 2006, was ready. To the credit of its German makers, it was a perfect fit, although its great weight compacted the trackbed outside the Hopetown Works; this meant that *Tornado* had to be encouraged back under cover with a forklift truck pulling and Land Rovers pushing.

Finance, even at this late stage, remained a constant concern. The boiler had been funded through a half-million pound bond and the tender by a single £200,000 donation from William Cook Cast Products, but although, by May 2008, £2.5 million had been raised, and spent, project costs were running at £10,000 a month. The price of steel was rising in line with the ambitions of the Chinese economy, and, although confident to the last, the Trust had much to think about beyond the sheer pleasure of witnessing the construction process draw to an end. Even when the locomotive was completed, it would still need to raise more than £800,000 to service loans and bond issues. With typical pluck, Chairman Mark Allatt said, "Our business plan shows that if, as long as we continue operating the tours we've planned to, and our convenantors – who have been so generous over so long – stick with us, we can pay that back, and, the quicker we pay that back, the quicker we can start building a new engine." *Tornado* carries a plaque with the following, heartfelt message: "This locomotive was built and paid for by people who shared a vision and were determined to turn it into reality." They did.

The boiler passed its hydraulic test – pressed to 360psi – at the beginning of 2008. On 9th January, Dorothy Mather, dressed in a fire-red jacket, lit the fire for the first time; the coal for the fire had been shovelled through the firebox door by Malcolm Crawley, a one-time premium apprentice at Doncaster under Peppercorn, and now a Vice-President of the A1 Trust and Chairman of the Gresley Society. Over the next 48 hours, steam was raised very slowly, and egg and bacon for sandwiches cooked on the shovel, until, at last, the safety valves lifted as a shock of steam, at 260psi – ten pounds above her normal maximum working pressure – resounded through the streets of terraced houses facing the Hopetown works. *Tornado* was alive.

The boiler made steam so very quickly, that the planned water supply was soon in danger of running out. A call was made to the local fire brigade who came to the rescue. Cooled down, the boiler was now insulated, clad and capped with a banjo dome hammered into shape by skilled workers on the North Norfolk Railway. By now, *Tornado* and the A1 Trust had established excellent working links with traditional and hi-tech manufacturing companies, the railway preservation movement, local politicians, the national press and, increasingly, a curious public. And, yet, as David Champion is at pains to point out, up until almost the last minute, many enthusiasts had said *Tornado* would never happen. "Some of them didn't want us to succeed. It's difficult to judge

quite why this was", says Champion. "Was it because *Tornado* was an intruder from the present day? Was it because the Trust had been so business-minded with its talk of project management and bonds rather than spanners and oily rags? Had we been too vintage claret rather than real ale for comfort? Or was it a kind of jealousy or *schadenfreude*. I suppose we'll never really know, because pretty much all enthusiasts rallied round to *Tornado* once she began to steam."

Knowing that newspapers often never let the facts get in the way of a good story, an amusing report of the first steaming appeared in the following day's edition of the *Northern Echo*, culminating with its editor having a face redder than both *Tornado's* first stokers and the colour of a fire engine supplied by the local brigade. 'Firefighters steam to save locomotion from exploding'... blasted the pyrotechnic five-column headline, suggesting that the A1 Trust had called 999 to avoid a calamitous disaster, when the fire brigade had simply ambled along after being asked if they could top up the water supply. Photographs of the incident, with white steam coming from *Tornado's* safety valves digitally retouched to look like black smoke, added to the drama.

"At no point was there any risk to the public, and there was never the slightest risk of an explosion,' said David Elliott later. "If the water had dropped we would have simply dropped the fire." The story did put local residents on red alert however, and after it appeared, A1 Trust members were forced to leaflet the area around Hopetown Works to put their minds at ease. At least it got the event noticed, and an extra bonus for the Trust was another story in the *Northern Echo* the following day to put the record straight, taking a positive slant and using words and phrases like "fantastic" and "phenomenal success". They came from the keyboard of a different reporter.

As a working steam locomotive, *Tornado* was effectively completed on 3rd July 2008, 70 years to the day that Gresley's streamlined 'A4' No. 4468 *Mallard*, with driver Joe Duddington at the controls and fireman Thomas Bray on the shovel, had taken the world speed record for a steam locomotive at 126mph down Stoke Bank between Grantham and Peterborough. This was certainly a time for celebration, but there was an intensive month ahead before *Tornado* could meet the press. This was because after so much mechanical engineering, the time had come to fit the electrics and electronics that were to make *Tornado* a steam locomotive for the 21st Century; she contains the most advanced electronics yet put inside a steam locomotive.

The man behind this hi-tech, digital side of *Tornado* was Rob Morland, the Trust's Director of Electrical Engineering. As Rob points out, computer and digital technology was employed early on in the project. All those worn Indian ink-on-linen drawings of the 'A1' from the National Railway Museum had been scanned into computer files and cleaned up on screen. Many were redrawn and others modified using computers, too.

"The wiring diagram for *Tornado* is more like a car than a steam locomotive", says Morland. There are 230 separate electrical cable runs, 2.4 miles of wiring and nine thousand electrical and electronic components. *Tornado* has two independent electrical generators, LED instruments and lighting, hazard warning lights, and the long-term capability of adapting to new wireless signals [ERTMS] out on the line. She's fitted with a National Radio Network radio for communication purposes, and even has a mobile phone charger!"

The twin generators ensure a steady and reliable electrical supply. There is a steam-powered generator and an axle-driven alternator on the tender. *Tornado* can also be plugged into the mains, or mains-supplied outboard generators when stationary or in depots. There are also batteries under the cab, affording a twelve-hour supply of electricity if all else fails. The original 'A1s' were equipped with steam-driven turbo-generators, but these soon fell out of use or were, after a time, simply disconnected.

Tornado is fitted with two safety systems. The first is the Train Protection and Warning System [TPWS] that applies the brake if the driver is going to pass a red signal; the other is the On-Train Monitoring Recorder [OTMR], an electronic 'black box' that records important operating data in the course of a run including boiler pressure, steam-chest pressure [the pressure of steam passing into the cylinders], speed and applied brake-force pressure.

The electronic control boxes for this, and other equipment, sit under the driver and fireman's seats. These are heavy duty pieces of kit, designed by Morland, that had to be able to withstand the rigorous conditions found on board an express passenger steam locomotive travelling long distances at 75mph whatever the weather. Electronics are rarely happy with dusty and greasy fingerprints; trying to imagine how they would withstand assaults by hot, wet coal dust and the hammer blows of an 'A1' at speed was, however, Morland's speciality. Military connectors, of the kind fitted to army tanks, were used to cope with hostile conditions onboard *Tornado* .

In practice, Morland's electronics have proved to be robust. Naturally, they need rather energetic, if careful, dusting, and yet they work well aiding crews as well as signalling, operating and maintenance staff. In motive power sheds, staff have been only too delighted to discover that *Tornado* is equipped with under-frame LED lighting. This means that maintenance can be carried at all times of day and in any lighting conditions with a degree of safety and assurance that were never guaranteed in the days of everyday steam. These lights can also be switched on to display *Tornado's* motion at speed by night. This was something the New York Central liked to do with the class 'J3-a' Hudsons [4-6-4s] that powered the American railroad's famous '20th Century Limited' express from New York to Chicago from the late 1930s to the mid-1940s. It must have been a glorious sight to witness one of these streamlined silver locomotives streaking through the night, wheels and motion spinning in a blur of steam-kissed electric light.

Tornado is also fitted with powerful LED headlamps – adapted from the latest operating theatre lighting, and three times more powerful than those found in the latest-generation cars – designed by Alan Green, an optical physicist with Sagentia, the Cambridge-based technology management and product development company. These hi-tech lamps are

The A1 Trust's Director of Electrical Engineering, Rob Morland, has equipped *Tornado* to cope with the rigours of the modern railway, this includes the latest safety and convenience equipment:

Opposite, left: The Train Protection and Warning System (TPWS) is one of the first lines of defence and automatically applies the brakes if the driver is going to pass a red signal.

Right, top: More akin to modern airliners than steam locomotives designed just after the Second World War, the electronic 'black box' records all *Tornado's* operating data, including speed, boiler pressure and braking force.

Right, middle and bottom: The modern electronics also include adjsutable cab lights, tender lights, front and rear LED lights, running board lighting and even hazard warning lights!
ALL: MATT HOWELL

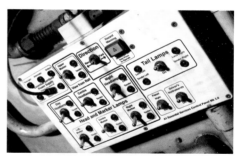

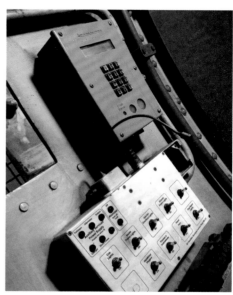

housed in traditional-style casings made by John Beesley. A further set of dimmable LED lights housed in the cab illuminate the instruments; these appear to glow – and very clearly indeed – as the locomotive thunders into tunnels, or into the night. Even though the A1 Trust has been negotiating 90mph running with Network Rail, drivers have no excuse for allowing the needle on *Tornado's* speedometer to sail past the 75mph mark.

Tornado was ready to move under her own power for the first time at Darlington. On 1st August, painted workshop grey, the 'A1' finally made her public debut. "My husband would be proud", said Dorothy Mather. *Tornado* would not exceed 10mph that day on the short, 500ft stretch of track leading out of Hopetown Works, but no-one could doubt that the 50th 'A1' was ready for the road. For those gathered at Darlington that day, it really did seem as if life had become a dream. Could this really be a fully working and full scale 'A1'? Could post-industrial Britain really have managed it? With a little help from the Germans, yes.

The singer-songwriter, Paddy Wex, was so moved by the sight and sound of *Tornado* that he penned a song, the first ode to a steam locomotive in what must have been many years. The chorus goes:

I want to see that smoke cloud
Take me back to the golden age of steam,
Where the firebox glows and the whistle blows,
Why, it comes back like a dream.
I love to hear those steel rails humming
To the song of the railway train,
And now Tornado *means we'll see*
One pulled by steam again.

The making of *Tornado* had been an extraordinary, and compelling, achievement. It had taken ten years longer than first expected, and the cost had risen from £1.6 million to £3 million. It was, without doubt, though, something to be inordinately proud of, and even to... sing about.

CHAPTER SEVEN

Tornado's debut
The great day arrives

August seems to be the month for special events on Britain's railways. *W. P. Allen*, the first Peppercorn 'A1', emerged from Doncaster works on 6th August 1948. On 3rd August 1968, regular main line steam came to an end on BR with the final embers being extinguished in the North West. On Friday 1st August 2008, *Tornado* was unveiled to the press and the public at Darlington.

In truth, and best not to tell everyone, No. 60163 had actually had been lit up for a secret run or two over the specially-constructed short section of track outside the erecting shop on Thursday 29th July, but then the team who had built it were entitled to a proving trip or two to ensure that everything would work properly on the real day.

It was painted in workshop mid-grey with the distinctly 21st Century legend *www.a1steam.com* emblazoned on the sides of her tender, surely a first for a steam locomotive, and certainly a clever marketing tool.

For the close-knit working members of the Trust, the evening before the big day was cause for a minor celebration, not with an excess of food and alcohol as one might imagine, but with a feeling of warm camaraderie that is usually reserved for intimate family events. For all the ups and downs of a decade and a half, *Tornado* was now a live object, and it was now only a few hours before the world's press would witness her in steam first hand, with hopefully millions viewing on the small screen around the world.

For the hardiest of the bunch, there was a 5am start, the time that a bewildered BBC Radio reporter arrived to conduct the first interview. The problem was, it proved nigh

Opposite: One in a million… the very first turn of *Tornado's* driving wheels captured at Darlington Locomotive Works before the official unveiling to the media on 29th July 2008.
TONY STREETER

A good job, nearly done. Chief Engineer David Elliott (seated front row, centre), is relaxed with arms folded, content that *Tornado* has seen daylight outside Darlington Works.
DANNY HOPKINS/STEAM RAILWAY

on impossible to explain to her how a steam locomotive worked, but never mind as she only wanted a few seconds of talk on tape. The *Tornado* press officer abandoned all hope of getting a satisfactory explanation understood, but at least the reporter did manage to grasp that the big long tube on top of the wheels was where the steam was brewed, and that it went down some long pipes to push the wheels round. How was it all controlled from the cockpit, and why was there a fire burning inside it? Never mind.

Other members of the media, and there were lots of them, proved far more knowledgeable, understanding, and genuinely interested. As well as the free tea, they quite enjoyed the informality of the Darlington complex, compared with the strictly-policed main line railway, allowed them freedom to interview and photograph at will.

The biggest coup for the A1 Trust was the decision of the BBC News 24 channel to bring a full outside broadcast crew. It all worked because nothing much else was happening out there, apart from a papal conference, which was hardly serious competition for air time. As the backbone of the morning's BBC programming, link reporter Robert Hall was expected to provide a live commentary, every 60 minutes, as the event gained momentum. The first run was due to take place at 11am, but the producer demanded its postponement by ten minutes after pointing out that the news bulletin had to be read out precisely on the turn of the hour.

The honour of giving *Tornado* a rousing send-off fell of course to Trust Chairman Mark Allatt, accompanied as ever by Dorothy Mather on his right, and watched by engineers, covenators, and media people. At 11.10am precisely, the drain cocks having opened a few seconds before, WHOOSH – *Tornado* inched backwards and collected the 'A1' baton that had been surrendered by sister No. 60145 *Saint Mungo* 22 years previously. Several key people however didn't see a thing, including BBC reporter Hall and Trust press spokesman for the day Howard Johnston. Enveloped by the clouds of steam in front of the engine, they had to give a live commentary, and both remarked afterwards that it isn't easy to keep the dialogue going for three minutes when you're standing inside an impenetrably thick cloud of thick, warm, hissing, white fog.

Some only just made one of the greatest events in the return to steam movement. The following morning's *Guardian* carried this author's news report:

"Please send *Tornado* to the rescue". My text message wings its way through the electronic ether from south of Grantham – where my two-mile-a-minute National Express Class 91 electric has been reduced to a 20mph crawl due to faults with the overhead line – to Darlington where, yesterday, Britain's very latest main line railway locomotive was turning its wheel for the first time in public.

"*Tornado* might well have been able to help. For this 160-ton, 3,000hp locomotive capable of 100mph is powered not by a fickle supply of electricity but by West Midlands coal, Durham water and sweat from a legion of enthusiastic brows. The end product of 18 years of fundraising, revived design skills and tenacious engineering by the members of the A1 Steam Locomotive Trust, *Tornado* will soon take to the main lines of Britain, and even of France and Germany, where it will rush trainloads of enthusiasts and others nostalgic for the age of steam at, wherever possible, a steady 90mph.

"Yesterday... it was the trim and perennially stylish Dorothy Mather, 92-year-old widow of Arthur Peppercorn under whose direction the original 'A1' Pacifics were designed at Doncaster, 75 miles south of Darlington, who set *Tornado's* banshee whistle screaming as Graeme Bunker... eased the locomotive away from the shed it had been built in at the old Stockton and Darlington Hopetown Carriage Works. "Absolutely marvellous", said Mather. "Bloody fantastic", said Bunker.

The Guardian even wrote a leader article the same day remarking on how modern railway management had "underestimated the British love of the past – and the emotional pull of steam, which is a vibrant thing compared with the robotic predictability of modern travel... No-one can doubt the commitment of the enthusiasts who raised £3 million to build it, or the pleasure that people will get from travelling at up to 90mph behind a steam engine. Some might wonder, though, whether Britain's love of past glories has come at a price: a country that can recreate its old trains lags behind the rest of Europe in adopting the best and fastest of the new. France has the TGV. England loves steam."

It does. As Mark Allatt said on the day, "the great thing about *Tornado* is that the project has involved people from all walks of life, old and new technologies, and its nurtured tremendous affection, bordering on love." The very love that had almost been forbidden those few decades earlier when BR banned steam, as if forever. *The Guardian* leader article drew the usual catty comments from the online 'community'. "Another perfect example of us looking back" squealed one of its many unkind members. "As my mother used to say 'God help us and save us'."

By contrast, another wrote: "Having a first-rate rail system and having a place for steam engines is not incompatible. A salute to those who made the new engine possible." A third, though, possibly hit the nail on the head. "If the politicians who controlled the railways of this country over much of the last 50 years had put as much passion into creating a modern railway as the A1 people have put into their locomotive, we would have a railway system that would lead the world."

We didn't, and haven't, yet on that August morning we did have No. 60163 *Tornado*. The BBC filmed her for news reports. BBC Radio gave her air time. Local and national media, from the *Newcastle Journal* to the *Wigan Evening Post* and from *The Sun* to *The Daily Telegraph* turned out in force. There was something about this powerful steam revival that clearly touched a national chord that day; equally, though, it was the story of the sheer dedication of those who had realised *Tornado*, against prevailing logic, against the financial odds, that was so compelling to the media. Speaking to *The Independent's* Jonathan Brown, whose much-loved Great Uncle Bert had driven 'A1s' on the East Coast Main Line from Grantham to King's Cross, David Elliott admitted to "harbouring a little anxiety" as the big day drew close.

"It feels a bit like when you are in the waiting room waiting for your wife to give birth for the first time," he says. "After all, this is the culmination of 18 years' hard work. Luckily, I have an extremely supportive wife. I never really have any spare time because even when I'm not working at the shed I'm thinking about the engine. Her view is that if I am messing around with this I'm not likely to be out chasing women..." Hardly. Elliott had been working 70 hours a week to get *Tornado* ready for 1st August. A former BR engineer who had moved on to building helicopters and hovercraft, Elliott had even moved from Cornwall to Darlington to take on the challenge of engineering and building the 50th 'A1'.

Unless you had a heart of stone, or harboured the acid cynicism of committed members of the online community, *Tornado* and the story of those who had laboured to create her could hardly have been anything but moving. Of course there was something a little crazy in devoting so much intelligence, business know-how, engineering and manufacturing skill, and sheer hard physical graft into the making of a 1948 express steam locomotive for the 21st Century. Yet, it is this passion that is so very moving. The love affair with steam was never really going to have gone away. It smouldered, simmered and then rose again. In Mills & Boon terms, *Tornado* had never been anything less than a steamy romance.

Reality set in again as once the media circus had moved on (although it was to return time and again in the following months), it was time to get *Tornado* into revenue-earning service. From Darlington works, *Tornado*, now registered onto the main line railways' computerised Total Operation Processing System [TOPS] as No. 98863 and with a 51A (Darlington) shed code plate fitted to her smokebox door, was transported by road on two articulated lorries to the Great Central Railway's station at Quorn & Woodhouse, and towed down to Loughborough shed. Running between Loughborough and Leicester, this is Britain's only preserved double track main line railway.

Beautifully aligned and engineered, and built to a Continental loading gauge, this was to have been Britain's railway link, via a Channel Tunnel of a more than a century ago, to mainland Europe. The brainchild of Sir Edward Watkin, a truly visionary railway entrepreneur, it never got further south east than London's ecclesiastically quiet Marylebone station. This London extension of the Great Central also had a very short life, opening in 1899 and closing to through trains to and from London in 1966, less than three months after the last 'A1' No. 60145 *Saint Mungo* had been withdrawn from service. The trains south from Nottingham through Loughborough and Leicester to London Marylebone had stayed loyal to steam to the very end.

The preserved Great Central, though, was the only line on which *Tornado* could get up to anything like speed. With a line limit of 60mph, it was possible to put in some of the 2,000 miles to "run in" the 'A1'. With approval from H. M. Railway Inspectorate, *Tornado* was soon running at 60 at the head of empty passenger trains weighing up to 500 tons. On one September run, *Tornado* climbed up the 1 in 176 gradient south from Rothley

A1 Trust Operations Chief Graeme Bunker has run up many miles on the footplate of *Tornado*. On 21st August 2008, he was just getting to understand the vagaries of the brand new locomotive.
TONY STREETER

station, producing 2,000 drawbar horsepower. She was beginning to flex her muscle. Inspectors described the tests as running "faultlessly" and "effortlessly."

Tornado also made her first runs with full passenger loads on the Great Central Railway between Loughborough Central and Leicester North. On the 28th September, she took well over a thousand of her convenantors and all those involved with the Trust the building of the locomotive in a special eight-coach train ending with a restored LNER pre-war streamlined observation car. The following day, No. 60163 pulled three trains for the public at large; each was sold out.

After these first, and very satisfying tests and public appearances, *Tornado* was packed off to the National Railway Museum, York, to be put on public display on the turntable in

Many agreed that the grey primer that *Tornado* ran her early trials in was quite attractive, and accentuated many of her final features. No. 60163 stands outside Loughborough shed at the privately-run Great Central Railway on 10th October 2008.
PHIL METCALFE

Above: The toast is *Tornado*. The brand new 'A1' was the sparkling centre of attention on the turntable at the National Railway Museum, the cathedral of steam, on 23rd October 2008. It was the star turn at the rail industry's flagship 'Dinner at the NRM' event along with four well-groomed Trust officers, Marketing Director Alexa Stott, Finance Director Barry Wilson, Operations Director Graeme Bunker, and Chairman Mark Allatt.
MATT HOWELL

Above right: In truth, Tornado cost no more to build than a modern diesel or electric locomotive, and may be just as reliable. Senior figures from the multi-billion pound UK rail industry gain their first view of Britain's newest locomotive at the 'Dinner at the NRM' event at York on 23rd October 2008.
MATT HOWELL

the Great Hall, the centrepiece of a major event and glistening under the floodlights close to some of the country's most celebrated railway treasures. The railway industry's flagship 'Dinner at the NRM' event was held around the locomotive on 23rd October, another chance for *Tornado* to make friends and influence people in exactly the right places: the nation's main line railways.

The next set of tests, to approve the 'A1' for 75mph passenger working, was carried out from York under the auspices of EWS. English, Welsh & Scottish Railway, formed after the privatisation of BR in the 1990s, was Britain's largest rail freight company in the 2000s. It was bought by Deutsche Bahn in 2007 and, two years later, EWS was renamed DB Schenker Rail (UK). For *Tornado* and the A1 Trust this was provident. Not only had EWS provided many of the main line steam crews from the mid-1990s, but DB was, of course, the owner of Dampflokwerk Meiningen. Its managers had never been as rabidly anti-steam as had BR's.

Express passenger steam locomotives in Germany had been kept in immaculate condition and in regular service into the 1980s, while DB has maintained a small operational fleet of some of its finest steam locomotives for posterity. Each year these are used on scheduled trains to the delight of enthusiasts. Steam in Germany might have been replaced, by and large, by electricity, yet there had been no reason to run it down either physically or intellectually.

Three principal test runs were conducted in November. The first, on 4th November, was from York to Scarborough and back with just the support coach in tow and under easy steam. On the 6th, *Tornado* ran a 142-mile return trip to Barrow Hill with a

500-ton passenger train at up to 60mph. On the night of 18th November, she ran the 176 miles to Newcastle and back at 75mph wherever possible. The sight and sound of *Tornado* screaming like a banshee in the night through Durham station and along past the city's owl-like cathedral tower at full speed, was truly enough to bring tears to the eyes of the stiffest-lipped men, and women, on the station's platforms. They may have blamed the cold weather – makes the eyes water, don't you know – but *Tornado* blazed through the Durham night, carrying the hopes of so very many people with her. Here was steam as the public had not seen it for more than half a century; a brand new express locomotive going through her paces and with a long future ahead of her.

On that evening, *Tornado* had run at an average of 71.2mph from York to a deliberate emergency stop, to test the brakes, at Chester-le-Street south of Newcastle. Assuming she had kept to an absolute maximum of 75mph this demonstrated her ability to accelerate a heavy train rapidly and to maintain the line limit as far as possible uphill, on the level, and downhill. This is far more impressive than climbing hills slowly and trying to make up time by racing down the other sides at very high speeds. The failure of the white metal of the inside and one of the outside crossheads, however, required the re-metalling of both, and an improvement to the way these components were lubricated. This, however, was a minor glitch and the fact that *Tornado* ran so very well out of the box impressed all those involved in testing her for main line running.

David Lacey of Durham was one of those standing on the platform at Durham that evening as Tornado thundered through. He wrote this letter, which captures the spirit of that moment, to the *Northern Echo*:

"Folks were lining the full length of Platforms 1 and 2 of Durham railway station, some standing two and three deep. A venerable gentleman leaning on his stick turned to me and said: "Thar's mair people here to'neet then when The Queen came." A little guy of five or six was bouncing up and down eagerly anticipating 'Big Thomas'. Then we heard the chime whistle. A bit naughty, A1 Steam Locomotive Trust, but so much more emotive than the weedy notes of the originals and somehow very appropriate. Again the whistle sang as she thundered across the viaduct and came into view at last.

"Cameras flashed and bystanders cheered as she roared by, spitting fire and steam. *Tornado* by name and *Tornado* by nature – the first steam train to be built in this country in nearly 50 years, which travelled from York to Newcastle on Tuesday as part of its main line tests. Then she was gone, as suddenly as she arrived. Smiling faces, some tear-stained, no doubt remembering days long gone when her sisters were a common sight and the world seemed a better place."

Tornado was returned to the NRM where she was painted, by a team led by Ian Matthews, in LNER apple green – with the legend BRITISH RAILWAYS spelt out in capitals, late 1940s-style, on her tender sides – and fitted with a lipless 'austerity'

It's always the attention to detail that impresses the purists, and signwriter Tony Philby shows that a craftsman's art is still highly valued. The cabside numbers and intricate lining were applied at the National Railway Museum's workshops at York on 10th December 2008.
JOHN HUNT

chimney. With a repaint in BR Brunswick green livery in mind early in 2011, doubtless to impress the 1960s enthusiasts who can only remember 'A1s' looking like this, there has been the chance to replace it with a lipped chimney of the kind her siblings would have sported for most of their lives. The aim had always been to turn *Tornado* out in a number of colour schemes both to reflect the history of the 'A1s' and to satisfy those enthusiasts who insist than she should be apple green, others who want the BR Blue of the early 1950s and those who clamour for Brunswick green. Mark Allatt, however, says that apple green will be *Tornado's* 'core' livery and that she will appear in other colour schemes for short periods only. One day, perhaps, the Trust might consider painting her BR rail blue with an Inter-City logo on her tender (with a yellow smokebox end and maroon bufferbeams?). Well, why not? It would be a lovely way of proving that the Modernisation Plan, and all its works, failed to rid the nation of the steam trains it evidently loves.

After spending Christmas 2008 under the public gaze in the Great Hall of the NRM, *Tornado* was back on the main line for a last round of main line acceptance tests in the New Year. After a perfect run from York to Leeds, *Tornado* had finally passed all the many inspecting bodies' hoops, receiving her certification to pull passengers on Network Rail. There had long been talk of testing *Tornado* up to a tantalising 100mph as, if she had been allowed to run at 90mph from the start and a ten per cent 'overspeed' had been allowed, then 99 it might have been.

With a nudge from a following wind, a slight downhill gradient, or even – surely not – a tiny tug on the regulator handle, *Tornado* might well have topped the magic hundred. Rumours in the railway press did, in fact, suggest that *Tornado* might have gone this

Far right: There certainly wasn't this size of crowd at Newcastle Central station in 1966 when the final BR 'A1' No. 60145 *Saint Mungo* made its final runs before going for scrap. On 31st January 2009, *Tornado* is almost mobbed as she makes her first main line run. With a few exceptions, the age of the spectators suggests they could have also been on the same platform 43 years previously.
EDDIE BOBROWSKI

Below: Not to be moved for a short while – the crew of Tornado pose at Newcastle Central on the engine's first run on 31st January 2009. No. 60163's brass worksplate on the cabside shows it was completed at Darlington Works the previous year.
EDDIE BOBROWSKI

Right: Newcastle United Football Club has a massive following, but not as great it seems as *Tornado*. Thousands lined the platforms at the city's Central station on 31st January 2009 to witness No. 60163's maiden main line outing.
EDDIE BOBROWSKI

fast. Recording equipment in the Class 67 diesel-electric freight engine she was towing at the back of 18th November test train seemed to suggest a maximum speed of 100mph. In reply, it was said that while the gearing of the Class 67 had been altered for passenger runs, the speed recording equipment had not been re-calibrated.

Whatever the truth, this had been a case of wish fulfilment. While it was undoubtedly astonishing to witness a brand new express passenger steam engine making its main line debut at the end of the first decade of the 21st Century, how much better would it be if it could be run at 100mph on one of its first ventures onto what had been the stamping ground of the original Peppercorn 'A1s'?

A big day for everyone was *Tornado's* main line debut on Saturday 31st January 2009, run for A1 Steam Locomotive Trust supporters, a repeat of the one hauled by the last Peppercorn survivor No. 60145 *Saint Mungo*, on 31st December 1965, not long before her withdrawal. The aptly named 'Peppercorn Pioneer' was planned to consist of 13 carriages, equating to about 500 tons, and will run up to 75mph. The timed departure from York was 12.07pm, arriving at Newcastle Central at 1.21pm, with a 4.34pm return trip, arriving back at York at 6pm. The trip was re-run the following day, 1st February, but concerns about football supporters marauding onto the platforms at Newcastle meant that the special only ran from York to Durham and back.

The first train that *Tornado* pulled on the main line, open to all fare-paying passengers, was the A1 Trust's 'Talisman' express from Darlington to King's Cross on Saturday 7th February. For many on board, this proved to be a highly emotional experience. For David Champion, *Tornado's* arrival at King's Cross was one of those never-to-be-repeated moments. "The platforms were absolutely crowded. The word had obviously spread far and wide. It took 40 minutes to walk from the back of the train to the locomotive. It was as if The Beatles had somehow magically reformed and had come into the station by train. The management was quite perplexed. I don't think they could imagine just how much this moment meant to the steam movement, and especially to all those who had willed *Tornado* into being for over 18 years."

Appropriately, perhaps, the first passenger trains *Tornado* worked out of London were a pair of 'Cathedrals Express' Valentine Day specials from Victoria, one for lunchtime and one for evening lovers; although whether or not the love expressed that day was for *Tornado* or human sweethearts, it was hard to say. Even then, *Tornado* was bereft of nameplates. While these had been cast years before, they were only to be attached at an official naming ceremony. With Mark Allatt, the Trust had typically aimed as high as possible for this event. It took place under the great curved roof of York station on a quite chilly 19th February with the Prince of Wales and Duchess of Cornwall doing the honours, and Dorothy Mather again in attendance.

Clearly impressed with *Tornado* and all the skill, effort and imagination – and above all, patience – that had gone into her making, Prince Charles has kept in touch with the Trust. A little over a year later, on 4th February 2010, the Prince and the Duchess had an

event to attend at Manchester's Museum of Science & Industry. The royal couple arrived by train from Preston, headed by *Tornado*. The Prince enjoyed his second footplate trip on the 'A1' as, after the visit, the train steamed away to Crewe. On behalf of the Trust, Chairman Mark Allatt received a letter of thanks from Prince Charles:

Dear Mr Allatt

I did just want to send my warmest thanks to you and your colleagues at the A1 Steam Locomotive Trust for once again providing such marvellous support during my visit to Manchester the other day.

It was wonderfully appropriate to use the *Tornado* locomotive to arrive at the Museum of Science and Industry and, needless to say, I greatly enjoyed my ride on the footplate late in the day. Please do thank Inspector Gareth Jones, Driver Bob Hart, Fireman Frank Sutton and Graeme Bunker, who all helped to make the journey a most memorable experience. I was covered in soot at the end of the journey..!

This comes with my warmest good wishes and heartfelt thanks – together with the hope that there will be other opportunities to deploy the *Tornado* on future Royal Train expeditions.

Yours most sincerely

Charles

The letter was sent on 14th February, Valentine's Day; a love letter not to Mr Allatt, but to *Tornado*. Conflating the romance of steam with Valentine's Day, Allatt had raised money for the construction of *Tornado* on the back of a love for the steam locomotive that stretched from the humblest cap-doffers (if such people still existed in 21st Century Britain) to the heir to the throne. Only the previous year, Allatt, the consummate marketing man, had been telling the pubic, "This Valentine's Day will be the last one when you can buy a part of a new steam locomotive *Tornado* for the man in your life. And what could be more romantic than helping to recreate the lost days of steam?" The ideal Valentine present for a man with steam in his blood, Allatt suggested, might be the sponsorship of ... a flexible boiler stay at £50, a large boiler tube at £200, a piston and rod at £1,900, or an exhaust steam injector at £12,500... "with other parts at prices to suit all pockets, however deep."

Tornado steamed north across the border into Scotland at the head of the 'Auld Reekie Express' on 28th February. But, as she clocked up miles on the main line, she was also a special guest star, as the Trust had long promised, at Britain's preserved railways and railway centres. This not only allowed many people to see *Tornado* close-up in steam and to ride behind her at a fraction of the cost of an excursion up and down the East

Coast, but also raised visitor numbers and revenue for the railways she visited. *Tornado* was proving to be a magnetic draw. She visited the North Yorkshire Moors Railway with its magnificent North Riding scenery and formidable gradients in May 2009, and the Severn Valley Railway in November to coincide with the school half-term holiday.

Quite how young people would react to a brand new steam locomotive had been more or less anyone's guess as *Tornado* was under construction. There had even been much discussion in the railway press in the 1990s about how the movement, and its locomotives, would come to an end as the last generation to grow up and to work with steam died away. It didn't. Steam locomotives are an elemental force; they appeal to young, old, rich, poor, humble and aloof. Schoolchildren love them. A bubbly young presenter of Channel 5 TV's *Milkshake* breakfast show for children was seen clearly enjoying a day working on a Great Western '57XX' Pannier tank shortly before this book went to press. If the editors of *Milkshake* like steam, the movement has little to worry about. *Tornado* itself has been a brilliant ambassador for the future of steam. In publicity terms, No. 60163 is a genuine star. One can even imagine the Thomas the Tank Engine team writing yet another post-Rev W. Awdry book: *Tornado, the Celebrity Engine.*

There were touching scenes when *Tornado* was displayed alongside the preserved Peppercorn 'A2' No. 60532 *Blue Peter* at Barrow Hill roundhouse at Chesterfield. The 'A2' had been painted apple green for the occasion to match No. 60163 Also on display were the 'A4' Pacifics Nos. 60007 *Sir Nigel Gresley* and 60009 *Union of South Africa.* Delightfully, *Tornado* was also lined up alongside the Romney Hythe & Dymchurch Railway's No 7 *Typhoon*, a one-third scale, 15-inch gauge version of a Gresley 'A1' Pacific designed by Henry Greenly and built by Paxman Davey in Colchester in 1927. The small, yet potent miniature Pacific had been numbered No. 60164 for its meeting with No. 60163. When new, *Typhoon* had posed alongside No. 4472 *Flying Scotsman* at King's Cross; in the intervening years, the smallest of these three East Coast Pacifics – the RH&DR runs from Hythe to Dungeness along one of England's most easterly fringes – had run without ever being withdrawn from service.

Far more touching, though, was the sight of *Tornado* drawing into London's Liverpool Street station at the head of the 'Winton Train' from Harwich on 4th September 2009. This was a 70th anniversary recreation of one of the eight trains Sir Nicholas Winton had organised, from an office in Prague, to rescue Jewish children from Czechoslovakia, sending them to foster families in England. Known as the 'British Schindler', Winton – then a 29-year old British stockbroker of German Jewish descent – saved the lives of 669 children. In England, they had all arrived at Liverpool Street's Platform 10.

Seventy years on, *Tornado* worked the last leg of an anniversary train from Prague Central Station to Liverpool Street. Covering a distance of 708 miles by rail through Germany and Holland, the 'Winton Train' was steam-hauled throughout. On board were 22 of those who had ridden the Winton trains between March and September 1939 and some of the five thousand descendants of those who made it safely to England. Very

Three East Coast Pacifics – 'A2' Nos. 60532 *Blue Peter*, 60009 *Union of South Africa* and 60007 *Sir Nigel Gresley* have met many times, but now they have a fourth player in the squad. New 'A1' No. 60163 *Tornado* joins a night-time depot line-up in this spectacular view outside Barrow Hill Roundhouse on 4th April 2009.
ROBIN COOMBES/A1 STEAM LOCOMOTIVE TRUST

sadly, a ninth train with a further 250 children on board never made it through. War was declared between Britain and Germany on 3rd September, and the train was stopped at the Dutch border. Winton could do little more to help Jews trapped in the deadly embrace of the Third Reich, although he served with the RAF throughout the Second World War.

When the Winton Train drew into Liverpool Street station, Sir Nicholas, now 100 years old, was there to meet it and its passengers. A young girl, dressed as she would have been seventy years ago, stepped down from the train and walked past *Tornado* towards the massed cameras of the British media. If you thought the scene at the end of *The Railway Children* film when Jenny Agutter, as 'Bobby', rushes to meet her father through steam blowing from a locomotive onto a [Keighley and Worth Valley Railway] station platform, moving, then this slow walk for the cameras was cathartic.

After greeting passengers, and being reunited with some of those he had saved, Sir Nicholas was only too happy to climb aboard the footplate of *Tornado*. This great and modest man – he kept quiet about his pre-war mission, until his wife discovered papers in the attic that hinted at the story in 1988 – proved to be a steam fan, too.

Without doubt, though, *Tornado's* greatest coup was BBC *Top Gear's* Race to the North. Originally suggested by Danny Hopkins, former Editor of *Steam Railway*, the race brought *Tornado* to the attention of a huge television audience. *Top Gear* attracts up to seven million viewers at home, and very many more overseas. Its 'in your face' antics and the boyish braggadocio of its presenters might not be to everyone's taste, but to see *Tornado* so admired by the programme's team and shown, on top form, to so many people who might otherwise have ignored or simply missed the locomotive, was encouraging. *Tornado*, if she had ever been, was no longer the preserve of railway enthusiasts; she was fast becoming a household name. The only other steam locomotives this can be said of are, perhaps, *Rocket*, *Flying Scotsman* and *Mallard*.

The trip was also an important one for dedicated enthusiasts whether or not they watched *Top Gear* or knew who Jeremy Clarkson was. This is because this was the first time since *Flying Scotsman's* exploit of May 1968 that a steam express had run all the way from London to Edinburgh. Many passengers on the ten-coach train said they had waited all those years for a trip like this. Although nominally non-stop, this special edition of the 'Cathedrals Express' had to stop four times to take on water – at Grantham, York, Newcastle and Berwick – and these stops added 96 minutes to the timetable. The actual running time was a mile-a-minute, or the same as the non-stop 'Elizabethan', a famous train of the 1950s and early 1960s, hauled – almost always – by a corridor tender 'A4'. The Peppercorn 'A1s' were never equipped with corridor tenders, to allow crew changes on the move, and were barred from this marathon run. Between 1937 and the outbreak of the Second World War, the 'A4'-hauled 'Coronation' ran daily from King's Cross to Edinburgh, and vice versa, in just six hours flat with a stop at Newcastle.

Knowing that the train would be shown to a very large television audience, railway management looked to their laurels. To ensure that *Tornado* was afforded the path of least resistance from King's Cross to Waverley, a National Express executive armed with mobile phone and radio communications rode the train, keeping in touch with signalboxes and train control centres along the way. *Tornado* blasted off from King's Cross in great style, storming through the narrow, damp tunnels up to Finsbury Park faster than most 'A1s' had done 50 years earlier – even on crack trains like the 'Talisman' and 'West Riding Limited'. Of course, there was a lot of joking on the way with Jeremy Clarkson suggesting that, if he died from all the shovelling he had to do, the crew should stoke his corpse into the fire for fuel, and there were the dramas of a, temporarily, malfunctioning injector and the inevitably uneven progress of a slow commuter train on the line ahead. Yet *Tornado* was, as we will see in the following chapter, to put up a very fine performance indeed, breaking several records made during the post-1968 preservations years on the way.

Tornado's debut year had certainly been a dramatic one. Best of all, though, perhaps for David Elliott in particular, the locomotive won a number of engineering awards, and

not least the Institution of Mechanical Engineers [IMechE] Engineering Heritage Award, presented to the Trust by the IMech E's chairman, Isobel Pollock, at the NRM, York in May. Graham Nicholas, the Trust's Quality and Certification Director, and a railway engineer with DB Schenker, spoke movingly of the combined efforts of so many people across the country to create *Tornado*. He explained how the biggest challenge he faced was dealing with this enormous sum of parts. "My principal concern", he said, "was how to gain approval for the locomotive to run on the main line. The process included having to embrace the modern regulatory regimes operated by the railway industry to prove the safety of the locomotive. Ultimately gaining that approval was the one thing that was particularly satisfying for me, and gave me a real sense of achievement."

Nicholas's experience had been repeated, in different ways, and shared by many different people during the course of the locomotive's construction. Bringing steam, brand new, hissing and roaring into a new century, and one in which the computer and digital technology were king and queen, had been more of a challenge than any of the five original founders of the Trust might have thought when David Champion drew up his battle plan for a Peppercorn 'A1' Pacific on a sheet of wine-stained paper 20 years ago.

Even then, there were those professional engineers who refused to be seduced. Responding online to the IMechE's announcement that *Tornado* had won its heritage award, Mike Bray wrote: "Sorry to say this, guys, but it saddens me to see such a waste of time, money and engineering excellence on an obsolete form of transport such as this. Our rail system has been under-invested and under-developed to such an extent that even now, in the 21st Century, we have to travel in cattle truck conditions, hauled by slow, noisy and highly polluting diesel engines. Electrification for many routes is a distant dream, as are decent tracks. Mechanical engineers are obsessed with the 'Romantic' past – get real; coal-fired locomotives belong in museums. I wish mechanical engineers would be more forward-thinking; it's no wonder the 'general public' think we are all geeks."

The experience of *Tornado's* first year demonstrated quite the opposite. The 'A1' gave mechanical engineers a good name; they were seen as people with souls who understood the value of engineering heritage, of why there is a wonder to be had in recreating machines from the past as well as the very latest technological marvels that might be dreamed up today. *Tornado* has also been a good ambassador for steam technology in general; far from being dead, steam not only produces much of the electricity to power electric trains, but a truly modern steam locomotive – an independent power station on wheels – might yet give the electricity and oil industry something to think about.

In any event, *Tornado*, and the older express locomotives she shares tracks with, have been immeasurably effective players in the long-term game of wooing passengers away from aircraft and even cars. The temptation to take a holiday by train, for example and particularly because the experience of flight is often so grim today, is growing. And, as *Tornado's* debut year proved beyond any doubt, a huge number of people are fond of steam. Today, these are more often than not the same people who are mustard keen on

Spot the newest locomotive. General Motors Class 66 diesel No. 66221, a product conceived in Canada in the late 1990s, is overshadowed by an immaculate *Tornado* on a running trial from York past Stourton (Leeds) on 28th January 2009.
LES NIXON

the very latest digital and electronic technology and communications. Just as there is no reason why letter writing with fountain pens is incompatible with sending emails by a laptop, or Blackberry, so we can have *Tornado* and Eurostar, Mk1 carriages trailing behind a chattering steam locomotive and triple-glazed, air-conditioned electric trains thrumming at three-miles-a-minute. And just as society tolerates ardent neophiliacs for whom the past is a distant country that no-one should consider visiting, so it embraces those with a love for the past, and can afford to indulge romantics. No-one, though, should be in any doubt, that *Tornado* restated the case for steam, even though she is not at the leading edge of steam technology, with persuasive delight in her first few months alive on the rails. Now it was time to see how well she performed on a demanding schedule of runs much looked forward to by the 'general public' the length and breadth of Britain.

CHAPTER EIGHT

On the road again
Surefooted as ever

Tornado stood simmering in London drizzle at the end of Platform 10 at King's Cross. It was a dreary Saturday morning in early May 2010. The locomotive was almost invisible, hidden by a crowd of enthusiasts most of whom would be travelling aboard the 13-coach 'Cathedrals Express' to York and back strung behind the apple green Pacific. Support crew appeared to swarm over *Tornado*, too, popping in and out their dedicated coach coupled immediately behind the tender. On the footplate, Don Clarke, Chris Bayliss and Jim Smith were busy making last-minute preparations. Clarke was in the driving seat, a veteran of steam from BR days, Bayliss (a driver, too) on the shovel, with Smith – the traction inspector – keeping an eye on things, and ready to help fire when necessary.

With three minutes to go, I was hustled onto the footplate and into the fireman's seat on the right-hand side of the cab. Almost imperceptibly, at 9.18am, Clarke wound the Pacific into gear and opened the regulator. He joined BR in the early 1960s and with just a few years to work steam; without a shadow of a doubt, Clarke and his colleagues, are steam men to the core. Watching driver and fireman at work, it was hard to believe that steam had ever gone away. With a rush of steam from the cylinder cocks – expelling any last water inside the cylinders – *Tornado* eased almost silently away from the platform and into the sudden, impenetrable gloom of Gasworks Tunnel. As we broke daylight again, and the rain began to fall, the quiet three-cylinder beat of the locomotive could be heard. With quiet confidence, *Tornado* accelerated easily up through Finsbury Park and the north London suburbs, waved on by well-wishers, the curious and the amazed as she got into her rhythmic, hypnotic stride.

What was so impressive was the ease with which the big locomotive set about her task. There was clearly no need to push the 'A1'. After stops to pick up passengers at Potters Bar and Stevenage, it was exciting to get up to 75mph and to stay there mile after mile. The coal was not the best, so although Bayliss ensured full pressure, thick clouds of coal dust whirled around the footplate, whipped up by a spitting cross wind. Whenever *Tornado* plunged into tunnels, it was a comfort to see its LED instruments lit so clearly. Otherwise the scene on board was reminiscent of an oil painting by Joseph Wright of Derby, the 18th Century English painter who, more than any other, caught and expressed the spirit of the Industrial Revolution. The crew, lit – chiaroscuro fashion – by the fire and swirling steam and dust, looked for those gloriously infernal moments like figures from Wright's *An Experiment on a Bird in the Air Pump* or *A Philosopher giving that Lecture on the Orrery in which a Lamp is put in place of the Sun*.

Tornado swayed gently as she cantered along past quizzical sheep, running horses and earnest photographers in fields, dismissing the dim world of supermarkets and shopping malls as she headed inexorably north. The crew worked hard – shovelling coal, keeping an eye out for signals, injecting water at high temperature into the boiler, hosing down the cab to keep coal dust at bay – and their unflappable calm was set in perfect balance with the storm of elements at work in the firebox, boiler, cylinders of their powerful mount. So many sensations, all crowding into the imagination at express speed.

Tornado picked up speed easily from signal checks announced by the loud AWS warning hooter, chimed through wayside stations and then, after a stop at Peterborough, worked hard for the first time since leaving King's Cross. As she approached the long climb to Stoke summit, Clarke finally opened the regulator, pulling the lever up to its limit. Now it was possible to hear the lovely low, insistent jazzy chatter of the Kylchap exhaust beginning to deepen as we sailed up the gradient. I would have liked these few minutes to have lasted an hour, although I doubt if Chris Bayliss would have shared the sentiment. Cresting the summit at 65mph, we plunged shrieking into Stoke Tunnel. Galloping back up to 75, we coursed down to Grantham signalled by the sky-piercing, 282ft spire of St Wulfram's. On went the air brakes, and we drew up in sidings close to the station exactly on time. To the very second.

I could have sat in that cab all day, but that would have been selfish. And lazy. What I had experienced for that couple of hours, though, was the thrill of riding *Tornado* at the head of an express on the very line Gresley and Peppercorn Pacifics were built to serve. In 2010. What I had not done, however, was to share in the behind-the-scenes operation that led to *Tornado* being at Platform 10, King's Cross, to greet me that Saturday morning. Graeme Bunker, the A1 Trust's Director of Operations, explained just what this entailed.

For that Saturday's run on the 'Cathedrals Express', preparations had begun on the Wednesday evening. This was when *Tornado's* fire was lit at Hither Green depot in south

Minus its 60163 smokebox numberplate (a new one is fitted for each journey and raffled off to raise funds), *Tornado* is prepared for duty at the National Railway Museum's running shed on 28th January 2009. In a few minutes time, it will be on its first daylight run to Leeds.
LES NIXON

east London. The depot is owned by DB Schenker, the German State Railway company that runs Britain's main line freight trains and provides crews for *Tornado*. On Thursday, as the engine raised steam very gently, cleaners got to work to ensure that *Tornado* gleamed. On Friday, an inspector had given the now-immaculate locomotive a thorough fitness to run examination.

In order to keep running, *Tornado* must have a constant cycle of examinations and maintenance. "Every time it goes out it has a 'fitness to run' exam by DB Schenker, one of two companies that can operate network-wide mainline steam trains," explains Bunker. In addition, the 'A1' Trust carries out a monthly 'A exam' to make sure *Tornado* will continue to pass its fitness to run tests and a six-monthly 'B exam'. "*Tornado* also has an annual 'C exam' by the insurance company and Vehicle Acceptance Body (VAB)," says Bunker. (*Tornado's* VAB is DeltaRail, which checks traction, is compliant with UK rail industry standards and have a mandate for working with steam locomotives.) All these examinations cover both the mechanical parts and the electrical system.

With a thumbs-up from the inspector, coal had been loaded into the tender, in this case a 7½ ton load from Russia (Scotland and the West Midlands are alternative sources). A hydrant at the depot was used to top up the water, although as Bunker says, "a garden hosepipe will do, as long as we've got the time." Then, more cleaning. "When *Tornado* goes out, it's showtime", says Bunker. "At a pinch, just one person can prepare the engine, but it takes an enormous effort to make it shine, especially if it's been on a run the previous day."

At 6am on Saturday morning, *Tornado* had finally left Hither Green, making its slowly to King's Cross around south London, and then up through Olympia and Gospel Oak to join the East Coast Main Line at Hornsey. United with its train, it had reversed this down to King's Cross with a diesel at the other end to act as a guide. When *Tornado* returned to King's Cross at 9.30pm that evening, she had to be taken back to Hither Green the same way that she had come that morning and "put to bed". "The day ends after midnight", says Bunker.

Because express steam locomotives are, in every way, 'specials', it takes an enormous effort to keep them in service. *Tornado*, which has now run well over of 25,000 miles, has been a goodwill ambassador for the steam movement; impeccably maintained, she runs without fuss and, nearly always, to time. Her ability to keep up a steady maximum speed over many miles makes her something of a favourite among railway management.

With her enhanced water capacity, *Tornado* is able to make longer runs than preserved express passenger locomotives; this allows her, for example, to run non-stop if need be from London to Grantham. "We can go 100 to 110 miles with a full tender", says Bunker, "which is around 20 miles more than most other engines. We very rarely go far enough to use a tender full of coal, but water is all important. Other engines would need to make three water stops between London and Newcastle, but now we'd only need two, and this helps make the journey times quicker."

As the water columns that were once a common feature of platform ends on Britain's railways and the water troughs set between tracks along main lines no longer exist, private tanker companies are hired to fill *Tornado's* tender during water stops, and not the Fire Brigade as is often thought. "The fire brigade only carry about 500 gallons of water in a single fire tender", says Bunker, "and we use over 6,000." At every stop-off, the engine is also oiled, filled with coal, and has its grate cleaned to remove metallic impurities from the coal that can stop air getting through to the fire.

Although working *Tornado* is clearly a harder assignment than driving a modern diesel or electric, the 'A1' is a favourite among crews as well as with a new generation of enthusiasts and railway operating management. Crews are employed by DB Schenker. They are all volunteers paid standard rates, working diesels on heavy freight trains one day, *Tornado* the next. There is, as yet, no shortage of steam crews, nor is the A1 Trust unduly concerned. "The great thing about *Tornado*", says Bunker – the 36-year old managing director of Steam Dreams, and indefatigable fireman – "is that she appeals to

It's an arduous task keeping a hungry Pacific steam locomotive fed. While running on the main line is the greatest challenge, *Tornado* still needs attention on depot, when it can be alight often for several days. A1 Trust regular Jon Pridmore is on the late shift at the Mid-Hants Railway on 31st August 2010, preparing *Tornado* for an early start the next day.
MATT HOWELL

young people as much she does to traditional enthusiasts. I love the fact that we see teenage girls photographing *Tornado* at stations with mobile phones and texting the images to friends. It means we're not up against an age barrier. It's the same with the crews; I think there'll always be people hooked on steam."

Out on the main line, *Tornado* has a decidedly youthful spring in her step. Without question, her performance has been highly impressive. Luckily, the A1 Trust has enjoyed the diligent services of Mike Notley, a highly experienced and precise train timer who, since Tornado first set wheels on the main line, has been keeping detailed logs of the runs she had made over main lines up and down the country. What these reveal is just how precise a tool *Tornado* is. Like the superb French compound Pacifics either designed or rebuilt by Andre Chapelon, No. 60163 is able to maintain her maximum permitted speed wherever and whenever possible. For the first time in the history of steam running in Britain since 1968, it has been possible to schedule trains with 60mph – a mile-a-minute – average speeds even over quite short distances. This might not sound terribly

Tornado has already covered the length and breadth of Britain, and the Cumbrian Coast Line offers some of most spectacular and varied scenery. No. 60163 is heading there on 10th April 2010 on the 'Cumbrian Coast Tornado'; the red headboard contrasts well with the apple green locomotive.
PHIL METCALFE

We've got there! This is a passenger's view of No. 60163 as it passes Parton on the same 'Cumbrian Coast Tornado' excursion on 10th April 2010.
EDDIE BOBROWSKI

fast today when even British trains are able to cruise for long distances at 125mph and Eurostars streak through Kent and across the plains of Northern France at 186mph [300km/h], but given an imposed 75mph speed limit, *Tornado* has little opportunity to average much faster than 60mph, especially as this average speed is achieved with the locomotive pulling long and heavy trains. Where – Eurostar excepted – many British express trains are made up of no more than eight or nine carriages, the 'Cathedrals Express', one of *Tornado's* regular turns, is normally composed of 13 coaches weighing upwards of 500 tons. In Britain, a passenger train weighing 500 tons is considered to be very heavy.

According to Mike Notley, "No. 60163's achievements in her first 18 months of service are little short of remarkable. That she should run so well 'straight out of the box' is a tribute to everyone involved in her construction. Eighteen 'even time' [mile-a-minute] start-to-stop runs in 2009 is a figure never before approached by any preserved steam locomotive. She is the 50th 'A1' and, as such, can only be expected to perform within the design parameters of the class. Therefore, her upper power limit is pre-defined in the 2,600-2,800ihp range and she is never going to match locomotives like the 'Duchess Coronations' and 'The Duke' [of Gloucester] for extreme short term power. Where she will be competitive, and this has already been proved, is on the longer high-speed climbs like Stoke, and to a slightly lesser extent, the Grayrigg/Shap combination in the North West of England. Here, the ability of her boiler to achieve and sustain a high steam rate with one fireman allows her to produce a big effort for long periods.

"Given the amount of work she has got through in the last 21 months [to August 2010], she must now be considered to be run-in. Some early teething problems have been overcome by fine tuning and she is now a better steam locomotive than she was 18 months ago. Her DB Schenker crews have gone through a steepish learning curve and we are now seeing the benefits of that process. Given that No. 60163 is working within the mandatory 75mph envelope, I consider that her regular work with 500-ton trailing loads on the East Coast Main Line and elsewhere is more demanding than her general workload would have been 50 to 60 years ago.

"As far as the future is concerned, I don't think that we will see any significant increase in her upper power range, rather that what she does will be done with even greater efficiency. Her coal and water consumption are already the envy of other large locomotives and give her an increased range between water stops that can only be achieved by other locomotives with the use of ancillary vehicles involving extra, non-commercial weight. Having taken a near 500-ton trailing load over Stoke at a minimum of 73mph on 14th August 2010, there is little scope for significant improvement without a relaxation of the upper speed limit. *Tornado*, to the public at large, is main line steam and has established herself as the flagship of the movement. She has taken preserved main line performance to another dimension."

This is a measured, yet terrific endorsement of *Tornado's* ability. No one doubts that No. 60163 can run readily, and happily, at 90mph over long distances, and, yes, with little extra effort she could exceed 100mph down Stoke Bank towards Peterborough and, indeed, elsewhere. This would be a great attraction, and adventure, for steam enthusiasts worldwide, but will it happen? The A1 Trust itself is keen to put *Tornado* through her paces.

"We will have to apply for a derogation [reduction of normal regulatory standards] as the current railway legislation limits the maximum speed for steam locomotives to 75mph," says David Elliott. This is mainly because of the age of preserved locomotives, although there are other considerations. "We have to looks at issues like the impact forces over bridges and on structures," says Graeme Bunker. "*Tornado* is no more aggressive in terms of what it does to the track than modern locomotives, but the weight is more concentrated and the entire 170 tons can end up on one bridge. We'll also need to ensure drivers have got adequate time to observe signals, as visibility from a modern

Tornado is no slouch when she is allowed to do what she was built for. Newark on the East Coast Main Line was regularly visited by most of the production 'A1s', and No. 60163 carries on the tradition in fine style.
SIMON LATHLANE

train is much better than from a steam engine. Higher speed also means more maintenance; we reckon that a 20 per cent increase in speed on a regular basis would mean a more than 40 per cent increase in wear and tear."

So, no, *Tornado* will not be making an attempt on 'A4' No. 4468 *Mallard's* 1938 world speed record, although, if costs can be met and railway operating rules relaxed, No. 60163 may well be running at up to 90mph in years to come. On the footplate, it is instructive to witness just how much of the time *Tornado* is running under easy steam, or no steam at all. Mike Notley's detailed logs reveal a locomotive that makes light of the tasks she is called on to perform. More so, they record performances that, despite the 75mph speed limit, are up there with some of the very best.

Under the spotlights of BBC television cameras, *Tornado* performed very well indeed on *Top Gear's* Race to the North on 25th April 2009. As far as the four hundred passengers on board were concerned, this was a normal run, as far as any express passenger steam train all the way from King's Cross to Edinburgh is normal at the end of the first decade of the 21st Century. With a ten-coach load of 375 tons, and with Don Clarke, Chris Bayliss and Jim Smith in charge on the footplate – not forgetting Jeremy Clarkson as assistant fireman – *Tornado* ran the 105.38 miles to Grantham in 95 min 45 sec. Checked by signals shortly before Peterborough, the net time was a minute or so less.

Once through Brookmans Park, a little over 14 miles from King's Cross, *Tornado* settled down to a 75mph cruise. Fluctuations before that signal slowing, to 61mph, at Fletton Junction, were minimal. Back up to speed, *Tornado* topped Stoke Summit at 64½ mph. It is interesting to see how this compares with some of the best pre-war runs down from King's Cross when steam ran very fast indeed. Of course, nothing can compare with the press run of the 'Silver Jubilee' streamliner on 27th September 1935. The pioneer 'A4' No. 2509 *Silver Link* whipped her 230-ton train through Peterborough in 55 min 2 sec compared with *Tornado's* 69 min 11 sec, but the Gresley Pacific had been allowed to reach 112 ½ mph twice and to average 100mph for 43 miles on end.

Tornado, however, was certainly up there with many of the best 'A1' runs of the 1950s and '60s. That speed limit, though, held her back from the very best. Consider her time – 21 min 59 sec – from passing Hitchin to flashing through Huntingdon 26.95 miles further north along one of the fastest stretches of East Coast Main Line. This was beaten by production 'A1' No. 60123 *H. A. Ivatt* (the first withdrawal in 1962) on a normal run recorded by W. Alan-Parker on board the morning 'West Riding' one day in the late 1950s, when, loaded to 360 tons, and starting from a scheduled stop at Hitchin, the older engine made the run in ten seconds less. This might not sound very much, but steam locomotives with large driving wheels take a while to get up to speed. The difference in the two performances is that, once in her stride, *H.A. Ivatt* was able to maintain 85-88mph. *Silver Link*, as matter of record, had covered the same section, pass-to-pass, in 15min 27 sec...

Working south from Carlisle over Shap Fell – the stamping ground of the LMS Stanier Pacifics – on 10th October 2009 with the 'Cumbrian Mountain Tornado', and towing 13

Jeremy Clarkson after *Top Gear's* Race to the North against a 1949 Jaguar car and a 1949 Vincent motorcycle. The renowned motoring journalist loved his time on *Tornado's* footplate.
JONATHAN GOURLAY

coaches weighing 505 tons, *Tornado* climbed up to Shap summit – 31.49 gruelling miles – in 39 min 4 sec, clearing the summit at 48½ mph. She might have done better on drier track; as it was she slipped with speed falling as low as 31mph. This, though, was up to normal 'Duchess Coronation' standards. A typical run from 1954 shows No. 46233 *Duchess of Sutherland*, now happily preserved and very much in steam, taking a 495-ton load to the same point high on the wind-blasted Cumbrian fells, in 39 min 20 sec. When really asked to perform, an LMS Pacific is, quite simply, that bit more powerful than an 'A1', however well fettled.

On a famous test run on 26th February 1939, No. 6234 *Duchess of Abercorn* charged up to Shap from Carlisle in 40 min 15 sec with a 20-car train of no less than 610 tons. On the way up the hillsides, and in driving snow, the 'Duchess Coronation' maintained between 3,021 and 3,348ihp, a British record. Over shorter distances, and in preservation, her sister No. 46229 *Duchess of Hamilton* has exerted over 3,500ihp on at least three separate occasions.

Heading north from Preston to Carlisle at the head of the 'Border Raider' on 24th June 2010, with 13 coaches and 480 tons, *Tornado* did very well indeed to run the 90.07 miles to Carlisle over the steeper ascent of Shap – four miles at 1 in 75 is a formidable challenge – as well as the earlier climb to Grayrigg, in 87 min 34 sec, or 61.7mph. This would have been first class work with a 'Duchess Coronation'. Significantly, while O. S. Nock recorded a very similar time in early 1964 with No. 46228 *Duchess of Rutland* on the 'Midday Scot' (which had rescued a Type 4 diesel at Crewe), the Stanier Pacific fell away to just 30mph over Shap – it was drizzling and the engine was slipping – while *Tornado* was over the top at 42½ mph. Just before losing it at Lambrigg Crossing, she produced a peak of what must have been close to 2,800ihp.

Tornado's proved to be the third fastest ascent of Shap by steam in the preservation era. The blue riband is held by the Peppercorn 'A2' No. 60532 *Blue Peter*, which climbed from the foot of Grayrigg to Shap summit in March 1998 at an average speed of 63.4mph, without speed falling below 54mph. "In the opinion of many", says Mike Notley, "myself included, the ultimate test of strength and endurance for a big locomotive is the long climb from Grayrigg to the top of Shap." *Blue Peter* did extremely well, although her load of 385 tons was way below *Tornado's* 480 tons. The 'A1' was, in fact, just 41 seconds slower than the 'A2'. The second fastest run was by 'A4' No. 60007 *Sir Nigel Gresley* – five seconds behind the 'A2' – with a 370-ton train in April 1998. Here, the LNER Pacifics have been beating the Stanier versions designed to tackle these climbs over the fells with aplomb. If pushed hard, however, a 'Duchess Coronation' would be able to take on and beat these East Coast interlopers.

The one sad thing about this once magnificent landscape, made even more glorious for many of us by pluming steam trains, is the fact that for mile after mile this stirring line is mirrored, as if through a glass darkly, by the M6 motorway and its ugly traffic. And, although there is much to be said in favour of electric trains, the relentless overhead

Grazing sheep have no interest in steam, but the passengers on the 'Border Raider' excursion on 24th June 2010 have paid good money to travel behind No. 60163 over the West Coast Main Line. The famous Shap Summit is only a short distance from this location, Greenholme.

PHIL METCALFE

catenary does little for the look of the fells. Their majesty, however, is restored when *Duchess of Sutherland* or *Tornado* hove into view climbing with assurance and with enormous dining car trains in tow.

Over the highly demanding 17.42 miles up from Appleby to Ais Gill on the awe-inspiring Settle & Carlisle Line (the old Midland Railway route to Scotland), and again with the 'Border Raider' on 24th June, *Tornado* covered the distance in 22 min 58 sec – despite a slowing for works on the track before Griseburn – thundering over the summit at 50 ½ mph. In the early 1960s, with Class 45 'Peak' class 2,300hp diesels in charge of trains weighing between 320 and 370 tons, the scheduled time for this section was 32 minutes. The 'Peaks', as two logs published by O. S. Nock in *The Railway Magazine* (August 1962) show, could bring this down to around 23 min 15 sec. *Tornado* did better than the diesels had with a much heavier train. On 7th January 1984, No. 46229 *Duchess*

Thirteen loaded coaches are no problem for *Tornado*, which breasted Ribblehead Viaduct on the Settle & Carlisle Line for the first time on 3rd October 2009. The condition of the Midland Railway structure threatened the closure of the route in the early 1990s, but it was reprieved and is now a vital Anglo-Scottish freight artery.
IAN McDONALD/A1 STEAM LOCOMOTIVE TRUST

of Hamilton with a 485-ton train was over a minute faster than *Tornado*, and, at 53mph, a little quicker over the top in drifting snow, but given that the 'A1' was checked by permanent way signals along the way, the honours would appear to be even. The departure from Carlisle had been tremendous with the locomotive once again extended to somewhere between 2,700 and 2,800ihp.

Mike Notley is right to highlight the climb *Tornado* made to Stoke summit on a run with the 'Cathedrals Express' on 14th August 2010. With Clarke, Bayliss and Smith on the footplate and the usual 13-coach load (495 tons), *Tornado* was put to the test with a tight 27-minute schedule for the 29.09 miles from Peterborough to Grantham. She did really well to clear the summit in less than 'even time' and a minimum of 73mph, recording, in the process her highest output to date: 2,800ihp. While this is good, the famous 'A4' No. 60022 *Mallard* did even better on the 2pm King's Cross-Newcastle express shortly

before she was withdrawn in 1963 for preservation in the National Collection. Delayed by signals, Driver Coe of King's Cross was determined to get to Grantham on time. He did, with a net time of 96½ minutes from King's Cross – very similar to *Tornado*'s on its Race to the North. On the climb, *Mallard* sustained 80mph for most of the way, with speed finally falling to 78mph at the summit. True, *Tornado*'s train was 80 tons, or two coaches, lighter, yet the maximum power output was 3,100ihp, a terrific show from an engine originally designed to sprint along this lines with trains of no more than 330 tons.

However, a run recorded by D. Veltom on 26th September 2009 shows *Tornado* recovering from a 25mph slowing at milepost 88 on the climb from Peterborough to Stoke Summit (milepost 100), and getting up to 70mph – 69.9mph in the log – at the top with a 515-ton train. By milepost 98, *Tornado* appears to have been exerting 3,080ihp. Despite Mike Notley's wisely cautious approach to figures relating to speed and power, it does seem as if *Tornado* is a member of the very exclusive club of British steam locomotives that have generated more than 3,000ihp. What must also be said is that on many of the runs the locomotive has made at averages of a mile a minute with heavy trains, her power output has been in the region of 2,500-2,800ihp over impressive distances. Still, with its heavy train on 14th August 2010, *Tornado* had crested Stoke at the same speed as 'A4s' managed on the lightweight 'Silver Jubilee' and 'Coronation' streamliners of the late 1930s. Perhaps, though, one of her most satisfying performances to date was at the head of the 'Cathedrals Express' on 19th December 2009, a few days before she rescued stranded commuters at London's Victoria station and took them home to Kent in the snow. The 83.02 mile stretch from Grantham to York took just 73 min 8 sec, including a severe signal slowing at Holgate Junction on the entry into York.

With Don Clarke driving as far as Doncaster and Chris Bayliss from there to York (the two men taking it in turns to fire), Mike Notley's log reveals that once up to over 70mph five miles north of Grantham, speed stayed above that figure – except for a single dip to 69mph at Egmanton crossing – until the train was slowed for those signals on the way into York. On board, such a long spell – over an hour – at such a consistent high speed is a hypnotic delight. It is hard not to feel that the train will continue to sprint along like this forever, and, equally, that this is the most natural way to travel up England's East Coast Main Line. This run is a credit to both locomotive and crew, the kind of predictable, dependable long distance sprint that keeps steam in favour with railway management.

By August 2010, the parameters of *Tornado*'s performance appear to have been set. Perhaps No. 60163 will nickel and dime her own records, stealing a few seconds here, adding a mile an hour or two there. What matters, of course, is that she can sustain such impressive shows of speed and power over the long haul. When, in 2018, her ten-year boiler certificate expires and she is forced into temporary retirement, it will be fascinating to see whether or not she will have lived up to her reputation as the best performing British main line steam locomotive of the 21st Century.

CHAPTER NINE

Tornado
the celebrity

Stardom is assured

After seeing *Tornado* under construction in Darlington in 2008 with his own eyes, the *Daily Mail's* Science Editor, Michael Hanlon, wrote: "The whole project is delightfully bonkers, so utterly British that just stepping through the doors of the workshop and getting a whiff of oil and acetylene, hot brass and stove enamel is enough to blow away the cynicism that comes from living in the 21st Century."

To the national press, steam had long seemed the stuff of 'Thomas the Tank Engine', puffer trains that went whoo-whoo, chuff-chuff, eccentrics (the human rather than the mechanical version), nostalgia, day trips for children in the summer holidays, Santa Specials at Christmas, and something to do with trainspotters who had existed somewhere back in the short-trousered, NHS-spectacled days of the black-and-white 1950s. When articles referring in any to steam appeared print, the journalist who wrote then would ritually declare that they had been keen on trains, much less a trainspotter. In short, the national press rarely took steam seriously. While it had been a tiny bit sad to see the 'old-time puffer trains' go in 1968, the general stance was "we mustn't stand in the way of progress." To wave the flag for steam would have meant being old-fashioned, inefficient and rather silly. Not even "delightfully bonkers".

If times have changed, then *Tornado* has done much to change them. In that same article in the *Daily Mail*, Hanlon asked Chief Engineer David Elliott a very contemporary, and perfectly serious, question. "What's the carbon footprint of this thing? 'I'd hate to think', says David Elliott. A quick calculation reveals that, by burning a hundredweight of coal every two and a half miles, *Tornado* churns out – in modern emissions – about 15,000 grams of carbon dioxide per kilometre travelled. That's 90 times the emissions of a small car. Still, with the ability to haul 12 coaches at 100mph, the carbon footprint per passenger is still tiny compared to even the most economical car."

In the course of his article, it was possible to see Hanlon torn between painting a portrait of *Tornado* in old-school, Fleet Street 'puffer' style, and writing thoughtfully about what this extraordinary machine represented, and why we want to build such machines in 21st Century Britain.

Tornado has become a prolific performer on the main line, covering tens of thousands of miles. The new-build 'A1' runs through Doncaster with the 'Cathedrals Express' from King's Cross to York on 27th November 2009.
GEOFF GRIFFITHS/A1 STEAM LOCOMOTIVE TRUST

The Settle & Carlisle Line is a beautiful route to photograph steam working hard. 'A1' No. 60163 *Tornado* passes Lunds on a 'Waverley' excursion.
SIMON LATHLANE

"Driving a steam locomotive has been likened to conducting a thunderstorm. Controlling a huge, angry animal might be a better analogy. It is nothing like operating any other kind of machine and feels like a mixture of a workout at the gym, a stint on a church organ and an exercise in concentration. Get it wrong and you will be killed or very badly hurt indeed. The controls, for example, are not the simple devices you find in a car or a plane or even a motorboat. Steam engines have to be tuned, coaxed, cosseted and occasionally threatened and prodded into obeying your orders. I had a go once, on a much smaller, simpler engine. I was exhausted after a few miles. How these men drove one of these for eight hours at a stint is a bewilderment."

"This was just a bit dramatic, especially to anyone who has ridden, fired and driven steam locomotives. They can seem a little capricious, temperamental even at times, and yet many – even the biggest – can be set to work very hard indeed with subtle input from the crew. That the experience of a footplate ride on steam locomotive is very different to that of any other form of mobile power, however, should go without saying."

In October, Hanlon was back in the pages of the *Daily Mail* after a footplate trip on *Tornado*: "It should be unpleasant in here, but for some reason it is not. In fact, it is quite the opposite, strangely comfortable, especially if you bag a spot on the driver's or fireman's seat. Maybe it is the sheer baroque beauty of the engineering on display.

"The sight from the cab window, along the boiler to the chimney and down to the organic, reciprocating motion of the valve gear, is mesmerising. Then there is the fire, which makes this more a living being than a machine. It is not surprising that steam engines are held in so much affection. They have an urgent, animal magnetism entirely absent from even the most charismatic diesel or electric locomotive. On one level these are just machines, relatively crude and inefficient devices, using Victorian technology to haul large quantities of people or freight along a track. Emotion aside, there is no logic in a return to steam on any scale; it is expensive, inefficient and labour intensive.

"But as any enthusiast will tell you, there is rather more to it than that. When I was at school, quite a few of us wanted to be train drivers when we grew up. There was still a hangover in the national psyche from the days when the men who piloted the great steam expresses were lionised, the most highly paid and highly skilled of the entire working class. But in recent years far more youngsters have fantasised about ghastly careers in football, pop music or finance. Money for nothing, an easy life. Flash car before you are 25 and on the way to retirement in your 40s. Well, who wants to be in finance now?

"If the era of silly money is truly over then, who knows, proper jobs doing proper things, such as driving trains and making things, may come back into fashion. I'm certainly glad I got my chance to make a fleeting boyhood dream come true, even if it was only for a few beguiling miles."

Hanlon was clearly getting into his stride. *Tornado* had put a spell on the journalist. You could stand back and watch as a writer who seemed to have been given a brief to write about old-time chuffers was warming to steam technology. Of course, he may well have been a closet steam buff, yet there seems to be no doubt that *Tornado* and the eighteen years of effort made by the Trust had caught the imagination of the media. In fact, some media companies started to go mad on trains. Where the BBC had barely shown a film about steam or indeed any railway matter unless it was to do with politics or, better still, crashes, since the days of *Railway Roundabout* (when 'A1s' were still racing up and down the East Coast Main Line), by the late 2000s, it was producing railway documentaries at a promiscuous or even a Stakhanovite rate.

Former politicians, editors of satirical magazines (well, *Private Eye*, anyway), ex-comedians, hand-waving historians and a raft of gurning minor celebrities appeared to be lining up like commuters along the platforms of London's Waterloo & City Line to take their turn fronting features, and even entire series, about railways. While this made a pleasant change from the seemingly endless home makeover, pave-over-your-garden, and cooking programmes, it could also be seen as a fundamental shift in the ways that railways were seen.

Not only were railways – and even *Tornado* in its own way – now being seen as far more environmentally-friendly than cars, and other forms of transport, but they were

A stunning classic LNER train – teak coaches hauled by an apple green Pacific. No. 60163 takes the North Yorkshire Moors Railway in its stride, passing Moorgates on 8th May 2009.
PHIL METCALFE

also being celebrated as a delightful way to travel, a way of re-discovering our history and even our sense of romance. While no-one has yet made the equivalent of Kenneth Clark's *Civilisation* or Jacob Bronowski's *The Ascent of Man* on railways, it really did appear as if the media's dismissive stance towards them, and to steam in particular, had changed tracks.

Michael Hanlon did bring matters down to earth, though, when he asked about sanitary arrangements onboard *Tornado*: "What do they do on a long run?" I ask. "Out the side, or on to the shovel and into the fire. 'And what about food and drink?' 'Well, there's a billycan of tea'. 'And they would cook their food, er, on the shovel?' 'The same shovel'." There can, of course, be no getting away from the fact that steam locomotives are elemental, even earthy machines, the very stuff, in fact, of the four elements known to the ancients: air, fire, earth and water.

Print aside, *Tornado* was the subject of many website reports, radio broadcasts and TV news appearances at the time she was unveiled to the public at Darlington on 1st August 2008. What was new, and remarkable, though, was the way in which she continued to woo broadcasters throughout the following year, and into 2010. "Indeed", wrote Michael Binyon in *The Times* in April 2009, "in its six short months of life, *Tornado*, the first mainline steam engine built in Britain for almost 50 years, has been a film star, splashed across newspaper pages and filmed in action by the thousands who contributed to its £3 million cost and waited 18 years to see an 'A1' Pacific locomotive running on Britain's main lines again."

What had also changed so very much since the days of regular steam was the way in which filming, broadcasting and the media itself had been democratised. Where the best-known films of steam railways at work in Britain had once been made by national bodies like the Post Office Film Unit [*Night Mail*, 1936], British Transport Films [*Elizabethan Express*, 1954; *Terminus*, 1961; *Snow*, 1963] and the BBC [*A Dog's Day Out*, 1952; *Railway Roundabout*, 1958-62; *Flying Scotsman*, 1968], by 2008, the rise and rise of the tiny, hand-held digital movie camera and the mobile phone with its ability to shoot "film", meant that anyone and everyone could try and be a John Grierson, John Schlesinger, John Adams or Tony Wheeler, just some of those highly-talented producers, directors and cameramen who had once brought steam alive with subtlety, grace and beauty. As C. Hamilton Ellis, the railway artist and romantic historian, often known to get carried away with emotion and drift into fantasy, said when interviewed by the BBC on board *Flying Scotsman's* 1968 non-stop run to Edinburgh, a journey by a steam train is "an aesthetic experience."

This cannot be said of many of the snatches of video placed on the YouTube website – the peoples' democratic film unit – and yet, despite all the shakiness and poor sound quality of so many of these films, the rustling of wind, the coughs and sneezes, the loud conversations in the background and the awkward heads nodding in and out of frame, there is something touching in the way so many people want to record their experience

To become a steam engine driver or fireman was the ambition of thousands of schoolboys of the past, and *Tornado* still delivers the dream, often at high speed on the main line. It's a grubby job, but a skilled one – and somebody has to do it!
EDDIE BOBROWSKI

of steam and to share it with others. The A1 Trust's website is chock-full with YouTube clips showing *Tornado* whistling through towns and countryside. The very mention of *Tornado*, especially when the timings of the trains she pulls are pinned up on stations along the way, brings a nation of amateur photographers and would be Cecil B. de Mille's out, on platforms, bridges and vantage points where the locomotive and its long trains can be seen and digitised to best advantage.

Professional camera crews were called out several times during the making of *Tornado*. The locomotive featured in BBC2's magazine programme *Working Lunch* in December 2007, and, the following year in Channel 5's *How Do They Do It?*, and in BBC4's *The Last Days of Steam*. Although the obvious temptation was always there, production teams tended to avoid the most banal clichés associated with steam locomotives in the media and to show just what a remarkable machine and engineering feat *Tornado* was, and how special the contribution made by so many people during the long construction

The Severn Valley Railway was built by the Great Western, but Doncaster-designed *Tornado* looks quite at home during a brief visit to the route for an enthusiasts' gala event.
SIMON LATHLANE

Overleaf: Photographed in black and white on the double-track section of the Great Central Railway on 27th March 2010, *Tornado* shows just how little has changed on certain UK routes in half a century.
ANDREW RAPACZ

process had been. The word 'icon', the bane of the professional journalist, was thankfully conspicuous by its absence.

On the day she made her public debut, *Tornado* was on BBC's *Today* programme. Robert Hall interviewed David Elliott on the footplate and was served a bacon sandwich – Peppercorn style – cooked on the shovel. "Who says there's no manufacturing in Britain?" quipped *Today* presenter Evan Davis.

The story was taken up in the Chinese, German and US press. When the Prince of Wales and the Duchess of Cornwall named *Tornado* the following February, the event was covered by *Country Life's* Octavia Pollock. There was something special, and very British indeed, in seeing media coverage for a steam locomotive extend from *The Times* to *The Sun*, and from *Steam Railway* to *Country Life*. Certain machines – machines that move – had captivated the media in different eras. Any list of these might include *Flying Scotsman*, *R100*, *Queen Mary*, *Mallard*, Spitfire, E–Type Jaguar, Concorde, and yet these had all been very much designs of their times. *Tornado* was different in that she appeared 60 years after her siblings, and yet she clearly caught something of the spirit of an age in which many people had begun to question the way our world was moving whether morally, environmentally or technologically.

There was something reassuring in the fact that there were people out their capable of making such a machine, men and women with skills that, in an age of floppy push buttons and electronic gizmos that could do many clever things yet lacked the slightest semblance of a soul, seemed increasingly heroic and worth celebrating. Perhaps only fundamentalist digerati and other unquestioning modernisers have failed to be at all excited by *Tornado*.

Media coverage had been important to *Tornado* from the beginning in ways largely irrelevant to the LNER during its ember days in the wake of the Second World War when Peppercorn Pacifics were rushed out from Darlington and Doncaster works. Those locomotives had been a necessity. They had no need of cheerleaders in the press to will them into being. *Tornado* was a luxury. There had been no need to build her. And she was always going to have been expensive. From the earliest days of the project, Mark Allatt in particular, first as Marketing Director and, from 2000, as Chairman of the A1 Trust, made plenty of time for the media. Early results were good. One of the first pieces in a national newspaper was as early as June 1993. This appeared in *The Independent*, and was written by Christian Wolmar who has since gone to write a number of best-selling railway books including *Fire & Steam*, *Blood, Iron & Gold* and *Engines at War*.

Of *Tornado* – although no name or number appeared in the article – Wolmar wrote, "It is the most ambitious project attempted by railway preservers. Although a team based at the Birmingham Railway Museum is in the process of building a Victorian 'Bloomer' engine, this is the first attempt to build from scratch a relatively modern, large express engine." The article went on to explain the "An 'A1' for less than a pint" fund raising policy, how 1,100 drawings had already been scanned into a computer-aided design system, and how the locomotive would, in all likelihood, be built in Doncaster. The 'Bloomer', was a recreation of one of J. E. McConnell's fast and powerful express passenger 2-2-2s built for the London & North Western Railway in the 1860s. The new Bloomer is nearing completion, after 20 years, at Birmingham Railway Museum, Tyseley.

The Engineer published a more detailed feature, by Chris Wheal (a freelance journalist today) in its August 1993 number, inviting readers – with its tongue ever so slightly in its cheek – to "Forget the Channel Tunnel and the Jubilee Line extension" because "the most exciting rail project in Britain is building the first brand new steam train for more than 30 years." Well, locomotive anyway. The article was based on what must have been a lively interview with David Elliott.

"He wants to meet the BS5750 quality standard and use computers and subcontractors. But he insists that all the work is done in imperial measurements. 'We use good old Christian English measurements and none of that foreign pagan rubbish', he says."

Wheal went on to discuss the serious issue of how the locomotive would be built given that the everyday heavy-duty engineering expertise and practical common knowledge taken for granted in the 1940s were no longer available.

"When locomotives were last made, tolerances were left to the experience of the workers at the yard. Any snags were sorted out by filing off excess metal. But as the new engine is being made partly by subcontractors, tolerances must be specified. Not British Standard tolerances, however. 'If you use BS Standards for everything on a steam locomotive it travels a mile, gets hot and seizes up', says Elliott. 'The tolerances have to be much sloppier than BS.' Take the coupling rods that join the wheels. A tolerance must be allowed for the moving bearings, and another for the wheels moving up and down independently on uneven track. Heat has to be allowed for as the boiler or firebox can warm the wheels to 100 degrees Centigrade. And a further tolerance is needed to compensate for the frame flexing as the train runs. 'In the old days, they found that if they made it a sloppy fit it worked. It is our intention to find a scientific tolerance.'"

Wheal's fascinating article ended by declaring "the loco will be completed in 1998." While *The Independent*, famous at the time for encouraging its journalists to write to their enthusiasms rather than to some more or less pre-set agenda, or simply to feature what all the other papers were covering, might be expected to find a story like this and to cover it intelligently and well, and while *The Engineer* had a duty to report on such matters accurately, it was particularly encouraging for the Trust to see serious coverage given to *Tornado* in the popular press. David Norris, Industrial Correspondent of the *Daily Mail*, wrote a stirring story on the project in February 1994 – and without once talking of 'puff-puffs'.

Of *Tornado* – by this time the locomotive had a name – Norris wrote: "Now it has fired the imagination of industry chiefs, who have seized on it as a chance to show the world Britain's engineering prowess is still second to none. Big companies are lining up to

provide materials and skills in return for having their names associated with the locomotive. And they are convinced that it will be the first of a series of engines, creating a mini-industry and jobs."

This was a little optimistic, and yet it showed that the project to build *Tornado* had lit a fuse within the popular media. This mattered greatly to the Trust because a key part of their approach to financing the new 'A1' was an appeal to anyone out there who cared for steam. It was seen as essential for the future of *Tornado* to involve as wide a spectrum of enthusiasts as possible and to encourage people who might have dismissed such a project before as simply playing trains to believe in the locomotive and the rewards she would one day offer.

Thinking of the long-term future was an all-important concern. Building *Tornado* would be one thing, but keeping her on the road earning money as well as delighting people quite another. In an interview with Christopher Lloyd of *The Sunday Times* in July 1994, David Elliott said, "We believe there is a genuine commercial argument for building new steam trains given the heart-tugging effect that steam-train travel has. In time, many engines that are being used on the 100 privately-run steam railways throughout the country will require replacement. Also, we can offer overhaul services, and mainline steam specials are a continuing commercial success."

This emphasis placed on the commercial aspect of *Tornado*, on finance and the long- term greatly helped the project's reception in the world of business and industry. While wishing to nurture a popular appeal, the Trust also needed the press on its side to help emphasise the rational as opposed to the romantic concerns involved in the building of No. 60163. An article in *Railway World* (August 1994), by Handel Kardas – the magazine's editor who sadly passed away in 2000 – was at pains to explain the ways in which two different types of computerised critical path analyses would be used to plot the various overlapping stages of construction. It described the quality of planning as sounding "mind-blowing", and very impressive to potential commercial sponsors.

"This opens the question", wrote Kardas: "of why any company should be interested in sponsoring the creation of a new express steam engine at all. There are it seems two answers at least. One is that there are a surprisingly large number of people in commerce and industry management who have a (frequently covert) liking for steam engines; the old magic is still there. The other, which has proved vital to several sponsorship deals is that firms appreciate the building of the 'A1' as a chance to firmly debunk the 'They can't build 'em like that any more' attitude that is so common in all walks of life. They are delighted to take part in a project that will show that British industry can still complete a heavy engineering project as well as it could 50 years ago. Better in some ways ..."

The message, firmly reinforced by *Railway World*, was that British management was secretly willing to help; what it needed was proof that the project was more than an exercise in pure nostalgia. Talk of critical path analyses could only help open the door to the nation's boardrooms. It did.

As well as main line outings, No. 60163 *Tornado* is making regular outings on UK preserved lines, where its capability is inevitably rarely exploited. The 'A1' clears its drain cocks at Bewdley, Severn Valley Railway, on 6th November 2009.
RICHARD HILL/A1 STEAM LOCOMOTIVE TRUST

The press, then, played a valuable and increasing role in promoting *Tornado* on a number of levels and to different audiences. There was a need to win widespread public support, to gain the interest of business and to encourage an empathetic response from engineers and other professionals engaged in design and manufacture. Even then, the media response to *Tornado* when the locomotive emerged from the old Hopetown Carriage Works in Darlington was beyond the Trust's most optimistic expectations. Far from being seen as the product of trainspotters mad about 'chuff-chuffs', *Tornado* was seen – throughout the media – for what she was, the end product of a dedicated construction process, a fine showcase for what survived of heavy duty British engineering, a happy marriage between old and new technologies, and, quite simply, a beautiful, stirring, soulful steam locomotive.

In fact, it seemed a case of plain steaming once *Tornado* took to the rails. The locomotive could do no wrong. So, when something did go wrong, how did the press react?

Sympathetically. Or, perhaps it didn't even notice: *Tornado* had become one of those success stories that, if they are very lucky, live a fairytale life in the media. No-one wants *Tornado* to have problems. During a layover, however, at Canterbury while running the 'Canterbury Tornado' excursion for Pathfinder Tours on 31st May 2010, fitters discovered what looked like problems with the boiler stays. *Tornado* ran back, light engine, to Hither Green depot in south east London, while the special was taken home by a diesel.

Tornado was back in action at the head of the 'Purbeck Tornado' on 16th June, running all the way from Waterloo and onto the preserved branch line, run by the Swanage Railway, from Wareham past Corfe Castle to the coast at Swanage. The BBC was there with Martin Payne, Commercial Manager of the Swanage Railway to say some nice things about *Tornado*. But, the 'A1' had to be taken out of service soon afterwards so that a total of 184 firebox stays could be replaced.

This meant the cancellation of a number of special trips in the summer, and not least perhaps the 'Torbay Express' from Bristol to Paignton and Kingswear and back on 11th July 2010. This particular special was important because Mark Allatt had built it up in the media as "the perfect way to escape the World Cup." *Devon Life's* Anna Turns took up the theme: "For football fans, the World Cup Final on Sunday 11th July 2010 will be the most exciting and eagerly-awaited day of the year. But many non-football fans are dreading the seemingly wall-to-wall coverage of the match and seeking ways to escape. The romance of steam is the perfect antidote to the 'beautiful game'... the 'Torbay Express' is the ideal way to avoid the day's football.

"The train, consisting of 1960s vintage carriages, offers full silver service dining in Premier Class and at-seat light meals in First Class, as well as its established traditional Devon cream teas. Off-train options include visits to the National Trust's Greenway House (the former holiday home of Agatha Christie) and the beautiful house and gardens of Coleton Fishacre, as a well as a River Dart cruise and a guided walking tour of historic Dartmouth. And not a football in sight."

Too good to be true? It was. This glorious press coverage was also, as events proved, an own goal for Allatt and the Trust, not all of whom are so passionately anti-football. Such future coverage, though, did express an unerring confidence in *Tornado* and her ability to perform on any given day. Allatt, however, has always been crystal clear with the media, convenantors of the 'A1' Trust and anyone involved with *Tornado*, whether a fare-paying passenger riding a mainline special or the boards of directors of the Trust's sponsors. This open-handed approach, while wholly natural, has been repaid through confidence, trust and understanding by the media.

Steam Railway's main line commentator, former Editor, and keen 'A1' follower Tony Streeter penned a worthwhile report in the magazine's September 2010 issue:

'A1' Tornado was back in action on 9th August – hauling empty coaching stock from Wembley to Eastleigh. That unusual sounding move was a prelude to the engine's return

Overleaf: The pefect chocolate box cover: 'A1' No. 60163 *Tornado* stretches its legs through the glorious scenery of Ker Moor on the West Somerset Railway.
DON BISHOP/A1 STEAM LOCOMOTIVE TRUST

to 'proper' work after replacement of firebox stays, starting with the 'Cathedrals Express' on 14th August. It was also, says A1 Steam Locomotive Trust Operations Director Graeme Bunker "a nice efficient way of working", because the coaches had to move anyway.

More significantly, it should bring a sigh of relief to No. 60163's many supporters that after six weeks the Peppercorn engine is ready to start earning money again. The cost not only of the repairs but also the lost revenue, says Bunker, is expected to be "north of £100,000." So, just how major was the work? How many stays were replaced? "The magic number is 184," he says. However, adds Bunker, "the reality is we haven't had a single broken stay. We've had tiny cracks, invisible to the naked eye. There have been five cracked stays."

Metallurgical tests have taken place, not only in Germany where the boiler was built, but also in the UK courtesy of the Trust's principal sponsor William Cook Cast Products. These have included non-destructive testing of the firebox. Bunker, therefore, says he can categorically dispel any rumours of wider problems: "No, there are no cracks in the firebox. People thought there were broken stays and there aren't..."

What next? By going for large scale stay replacement, Bunker says "we've tried to get as much fatigue out as we can," the idea being to "give ourselves time for more detailed, thorough consideration. The team has done very well and worked very hard," he adds of what has been a pretty major job – and once again the Trust is keen to thank Balfour Beatty for making its Hither Green shed available. Now, the 'detailed consideration' really starts: "How much is growing pains, which our boiler inspectors tell us it is?" Bunker says. "How much is learning about the boiler, because it is a unique vessel?"

With an all-steel, all-welded boiler, he adds: "In effect it de-stresses itself over time." Comparisons between the 'apples and pears' of traditional copper and all-steel boilers are difficult, he reckons, but "copper fireboxes have their weaknesses as well, because you have lap joints." Much more to the point, says the A1 Trust's ops man, is that with lots of steamings and 20,000-odd miles racked up by the supremely busy engine over the last two years, "in terms of what boilers are put through, it is working quite hard."

One big difference between the way *Tornado* and the previous 49 'A1' were worked is in the heating and cooling cycles of the boiler. In everyday service, the 'A1s', like most mainline locomotives, would be in steam – or at least the boiler would be warm – for days and even weeks at a time. This was so a locomotive could be ready for the road as quickly as possible, but also to prevent a boiler from heating up from cold and then cooling down again at brief intervals that would have meant it expanding and contracting

Peppercorn 'A1' No. 60163 *Tornado* is on unfamiliar territory, approaching Bunbury with the returning Steam Dreams 'Cathedrals Express' from Chester to London Euston on 22nd May 2010.
NIGEL CAPELLE

in uncomfortable and even deleterious cycles. Because *Tornado* is not run nearly so frequently as an 'A1' in regular service was, its boiler works harder for a living.

The Trust handled this minor crisis well, by pre-empting media enquiries with an open and detailed response to Tornado's temporary withdrawal from service. The repairs had cost £50,000 while £75,000 profit was lost from revenue Tornado should have earned through July. By the time Tornado was back in action, no-one seemed to mind the inconveniences they might have been put through. It was if a diva had had a bad throat and was unable to sing at Covent Garden for a few weeks.

Tornado had become more than a diva, though, for she had proven to be a darling of the media, a whistle blow for the common man, woman and child as well as a magnificent machine that haunts the imaginations of company directors, bankers, medics, lawyers, the Prince of Wales. "We were worried", says Trust Chairman Mark Allatt, "people wouldn't feel an emotional attachment to a locomotive that had no history. However, because people have paid for it and seen it growing before them, there is a much deeper emotional tie than we ever expected. It's also something children feel they can associate with because it's not a hundred years older than them."

Most remarkably, it was something the gentle folk of the media could associate with, too. With the coming of *Tornado*, they put away childish clichés and decided that a steam locomotive was truly a thing of elemental beauty and a fiery joy forever, and not one of the 'old time puffer trains' of Fleet Street yore.

CHAPTER TEN

The future

What should we build next?

Tornado has been designed for a long and hard working life. The steam locomotive in general is a robust machine and can be rebuilt to extend its life almost infinitely. In Britain today, there is nothing surprising in finding a locomotive of 130 years old and more at the front of a train and, in the case of the narrow-gauge railways of North Wales, these are expected to work very hard indeed as they climb the slippery and tortuously curved slopes of Snowdonia. Age does not appear to weary them.

The A1 Trust made it clear from early on that once it had built a Peppercorn, it would like to go on to create new locomotives. Having assembled such a professional team and sourced the ways and means by which a main line express passenger steam locomotive could be built into the 21st Century, it seemed to everyone on board the project that it would be folly to let all this talent, skill and know-how melt into the air – or vanish in a cloud of superheated steam.

The talk in the wings had always, in fact, been of building a new Gresley 'P2' 2-8-2. There have been other suggestions along the line, and yet the 'P2' has not so much simmered as hissed and roared its way for attention since the Trust was formed 20 years ago. Without doubt, the P2s, especially the first two locomotives – Nos. 2001 *Cock o' The North* and 2002 *Earl Marischal* – were among the most spectacular, and beautiful, locomotives ever built for a British railway. And yet, because they were converted, from 1943, into what proved to be the fast if slippery and ultimately rather ineffectual 'A2/2'

Pacifics, they have long been a kind of spectre haunting the imagination of steam enthusiasts everywhere. It was seen as another case of incumbent CME Edward Thompson wreaking revenge over his predecessor, and it came as no surprise that in 1959 they were amongst the first casualties of the dieselisation of East Coast services. In any case, photographs of these magnificent engines in their superb-looking original condition are surely enough to make anyone with steam in their blood want to see one working again.

In June 2010, the Trust finally went public with the news that it had started a feasibility study into the construction of a 'P2'. "The 'P2'", said Mark Allatt, "has around 70 per cent commonality with Tornado, including the boiler, tender and many other detailed fittings. However, the design was never fully developed and the locomotives failed to

reach their full potential... initial conversations with the regulatory bodies have been very positive, but we have a long way to go yet."

The announcement coincided with a statement by the Trust to the effect that, as of June 2010, it had halved the debt incurred during the construction of *Tornado*, and that the only remaining debt associated with the locomotive was the £500,000 bearer bond due for repayment by the end of 2016. *Tornado* was earning her way, and the Trust was confident that its cashflow matched the flow of steam passing through the 'A1'. Now it was perfectly feasible, and despite the recession crowding British finances, to look to a future bright with both a Peppercorn 'A1' and a Gresley 'P2' out on the main line.

The 'P2s' were the first, and only, eight-coupled express passenger locomotive in Britain. Gresley, always interested in big engines, had produced a pair of 2-8-2s, Britain's

The Gresley 'P2' 2-8-2s were built to haul big trains. Demonstrating that ability, first-built No. 2001 *Cock o'The North* heads a Leeds to King's Cross express in May 1935. She has just passed Greenwood, near Hadley Wood. After rebuilding by Edward Thompson as a Pacific, she lacked both charisma and pulling power compared to other LNER express engines.
C. R. GORDON STUART/RAIL ARCHIVE STEPHENSON

first, as early as 1925. These were the 'P1s', designed for fast and heavy goods trains. Gresley had, at first, wanted ever bigger engines, toying with proposals for a 2-10-2 in late Great Northern days shortly after the First World War. With their 'A1' boilers, three 20 x 26 inch cylinder and 5ft 2inch driving wheels, the 'P1s' could exert a very usable tractive effort of 38,500lb, boosted by an auxiliary two-cylinder unit on the trailing truck to 47,000lbs on starting.

That these were very powerful and effective locomotives, there can be no doubt. They were able to haul 100-wagon coal trains weighing 1,600 tons between Peterborough and London and they ran happily at 65mph. There was one small problem: trains of this length were simply too much for the operating departments to cope with and, by 1932, only one 100-wagon train a day was scheduled. The 'P1s' were simply too powerful for their own good. Even then they received 'A3' boilers in 1942, but by this time their rear-wheel boosters had been removed and these great engines, out of favour when Thompson took over as CME, were withdrawn in July 1945.

In contrast, the power and adhesion of the 'P2s' was greatly welcomed by the operating departments when they arrived in Scotland to take over the heaviest workings on the Edinburgh to Aberdeen line. This had always been a difficult route with precipitous gradients and screeching curves presenting daunting challenges to locomotive designers and crews. The 'P2s' were a revelation for Scottish enginemen. Designed to take 550-ton sleeping car expresses over this route, they made any locomotive that had come before seem not just undersized, but puny.

Six of these charismatic machines, designed with considerable input from Gresley's principal assistant, Oliver Bulleid, were built all bearing stirring Scottish names, from *Cock o' The North* to *Thane of Fife* and *Wolf of Badenoch*. The first, No. 2001 *Cock o'the North*, was a radical locomotive in several ways. Owing much to the research of Andre Chapelon in France, she boasted streamlined internal steam passages, a high degree of superheat, a double Kylchap exhaust, a massive fire grate – 50 sq ft – an ACFI [Societe l'Auxiliare des Chemins de Fer et de l'Industrie] feed water heater (a way of dispensing with troublesome steam injectors), and Lentz rotary cam poppet valves instead of the Gresley-Walschaerts valve gear de rigeur on LNER locomotives. If Gresley was in any way trying to create a stir technically, then the aesthetic of the new locomotive was as striking as it was audacious.

The sheer length of this determinedly modern locomotive was impressive, but with wholly exposed driving wheels – British engineers had long hidden the tops of these with low running boards and splashers as if naked wheels were somehow indecent – a V-shaped cab front and a front end that spoke of wind-tunnels and streamlining, *Cock o' The North* was a photographer's, filmmaker's and progressive-minded enthusiast's dream. She also sounded the part with her haunting American chime whistle. This was the very first fitted to an LNER locomotive. It had been presented to Gresley by Captain Jack Howey, the famous racing driver and creator of the Romney Hythe & Dymchurch

Railway on a visit the CME made to see progress there at the time the miniature railway was taking delivery of its latest, US-style Pacifics *Dr Syn* and *Black Prince*. Gresley was much taken with the triple-note whistle (made by Crosby in Boston, Massachussets), and when Howey made a present of it, he had it fitted to *Cock o'the North*. He ordered further chime whistles for the 'P2s', and for the 'A4s'.

Completed at Doncaster in May 1934, *Cock o' The North* made her appropriately impressive debut in June 1934, drawing a 20-coach train, including the LNER's dynamometer car to monitor the engine's performance out of King's Cross. With a tractive effort of 43,462lb, greater than that of its contemporaries, and its great adhesion, No. 2001 pulled this great train up through Gasworks and Copenhagen Tunnels with consummate ease. She ran happily, despite her 6ft 2in driving wheels – considered too small for high speed at the time – at up to 85mph, topped Stoke bank at 57.5mph and, on the way up the hill from Essendine, produced 2,100dbhp.

After a brief spell in Scotland, *Cock o' The North* was packed off to France in December 1934. With a train carrying her own stash of coal, No. 2001 travelled by sea from Harwich to Calais before steaming down to the new stationary locomotive test plant at Vitry-sur-Seine. Gresley had attended its opening the previous September. Here, under the watchful eyes of Bulleid and Chapelon, No. 2001 revealed several faults, some of which were rectified, although the A1 Trust will need to complete the task in years to come. While the locomotive proved free steaming, its axles, bearings and big-ends ran hot. In addition, French engineers considered the ashpan too small – restricting steaming – and the firebox door to be too small with the result that it was hard to cover the grate evenly with coal.

Out on the road, the 'P2' performed with a degree of panache, running well with a test train at 70mph while exerting a sustained 2,000dbhp. Bulleid, among others, claimed a maximum of 2,800dbhp, but this high figure was never substantiated. Back in Scotland, *Cock o' The North* proved to have the strength of Hercules on the formidable banks between Edinburgh and Aberdeen, although she had an almost insatiable appetite for coal, consuming as much as ten tons on a return trip between Auld Reekie and the Granite City. This was asking far too much of fireman, even those brought up with the coal-guzzling North British Atlantics that had dominated this route for many years. Passengers also commented on the sparks flying from the locomotive and the constant patter of cinders and poorly combusted coal along carriage roofs.

There were other problems. The Lentz rotary cam poppet valves gave problems, as did the ACFI feed water heater. There was rapid wear in the axle boxes, journals, side rods and bearings. Fractured pipes and joints were further complaints made against No. 2001. During Thompson's era it was even said that the 'P2s' spread tracks, although as commentator O. S. Nock wrote, putting the case for the defence, "in my footplate experience on several of them, they rode easily and elegantly round the sharpest curves, and never gave any impression of binding or of spreading the road... I felt this contention was largely propaganda to help justify the rebuilding."

Previous pages, clockwise from left: When new, the 'A1s' were notoriously rough riding, but *Tornado* is a great improvement on the original design. We are looking across from the driver's side to the fireman's area.

Heavy engineering, a modern version of an efficient design... *Tornado*'s left-hand motion.

The fire when *Tornado* is at rest. When the new 'A1' Pacific is working hard, this will burn white hot.

Tornado carries the original pattern high-pitched whistle, but also a chime version, discreetly placed beside the right-hand smoke deflector at the front of the engine.
ALL: MATT HOWELL

Right: Form and function in stunning detail at Ropley, Mid-Hants Railway. This is *Tornado*'s left-hand side.

Opposite: Not the inside of a ship's engine room, but *Tornado*'s cab. The right-hand gauge is the speedometer and if the A1 Trust can gain the necessary permissions we can all hope to one day see this touching 90mph on the main line.
ALL: MATT HOWELL

The pony truck, however, was unsatisfactory, putting undue strain on the driving wheels, and their crank axles and big ends as the 'P2s' pounded around tight bends. Chapelon recommended the use of the Italian Bissel arrangement that proved very successful in his supremely efficient '141P' 2-8-2s, and that might well be fitted to 2007, the A1 Trust's very own 'P2'.

Many of the problems were ironed out over the next two years. When *Cock o' The North* was sent to Doncaster for heavy repair in September 1937 it was fitted with Walschaerts-Gresley valve gear, as well as a streamlined, 'A4'-style front end, as *Earl Marischal* had been the previous year. The other four 'P2s' had been built in this fashion. Wartime clearly placed a strain on these magisterial locomotives. By 1942, for every day one of Gresley's highly competent fast mixed-traffic 'V2' 2-6-2s spent out of service, the 'P2s' demanded three. Inevitably, Thompson jumped at this opportunity to cut the six 2-8-2s down to size. In January 1943, No. 2005 *Thane of Fife* re-emerged from Doncaster as a rather ugly 4-6-2, a shadow of her former herself. The other members of the class followed; they were to be the first class of LNER Pacifics to be completely withdrawn from service in Britain.

In their brief heyday, the 'P2s' had performed superbly well on the arduous road from Aberdeen to Edinburgh over the Tay and Forth Bridges. They could could run these routes as quickly as the Peppercorn 'A2's did in the 1950s and 60s, but with loads with trains of 550 rather than 400 tons. These journeys included several stops and required tremendous acceleration up steep grades to keep time. O. S. Nock, who rode the footplates of both Nos. 2001 and 2002 in the summer of 1935, declared the latter [*Earl Marischal*] "the most puissant British locomotive I have ever set foot on." For ardent steam enthusiasts, his descriptions of runs with these locomotives are compelling.

On the 10.20am from Aberdeen loaded to 515 tons, and with Driver Arbuthnot and Fireman Conning in charge, *Earl Marischal* lifted her heavy train away and up the hill around the Girdle Ness lighthouse and past Cove Bay station in great style. As Nock describes: "Using the high tractive effort of the engine to the full, we fairly sailed up the bank... One thing impressed me at once on this grand engine. As on all modern Gresley designs a steam chest pressure gauge was fitted, so that one could read off the pressure at which steam was actually entering the cylinders. These runs of mine were made before the introduction of the streamlined 'A4' Pacifics, and on the 'A3s' and [Gresley] 'A1s' when the regulator was full open, as it was with Driver Arbuthnot on all the steep ascents, there was no difference at all between boiler pressure and steam chest pressure. This was striking testimony to the careful design of the steam passages and to the degree of internal streamlining that had been built into them."

Nock spoke of the relative quiet and ease with which the 'P2' performed its duty, of "plenty of brisk running downhill at 65 to 70mph, and of the "luxurious way in which curves were taken." At Tay Bridge station, Nock swapped the footplate of *Earl Marischal* for that of *Cock o' The North*, with Driver Sheddon and Fireman Hardisty of Haymarket

shed charged with running from Dundee to Edinburgh in 85 minutes. He reported the locomotive running at 60 to 65mph "entirely without steam" wherever curves and gradients allowed.

He became quite rhapsodic as No. 2001 approached the formidable, twisting climb up to the Forth Bridge "made all the worse by the slow speed at which it is commenced … And then every feature that had gone to make up the thrill of the day's running worked up to a tremendous climax. For one brief mile the big engine was working really hard. On the footplate the atmosphere was thick with flying coal dust; the smell of hot oil mingled strangely with gusts of keen night air. In the tunnel *Cock o' The North* literally roared, while little stabs of fire shot from the chimney hit the roof and rebounded in a shower over the cab.

"At a steady 19mph we came out into the open and so on to the Forth Bridge. The crossing was yet another unforgettable experience: a deep hollow reverberation from our wheels; once again the lighting of the cross-girders by the fire-glow as we passed underneath; far below the masts of the ships, and all the time the sharp staccato beat of *Cock o' The North* rising over all. Once on to the bridge, the speed quickly rose, but the engine was held in until we had cleared the junctions at Dalmeny. Then we were away in earnest to touch 68mph at Turnhouse, and to sustain a fast pace to the outskirts of Edinburgh."

Now, imagine what a trip like this might be like in years to come on a train hauled by the, as yet, unnamed No. 2007. This locomotive will have all the performance of *Cock o' The North* and *Earl Marischal*, and then some. And, 2007 will be, if the Trust gets its way, more efficient and more reliable than these 1930s originals.

Enthusiasts appear excited by the idea and web forums are already filled with comments on such a project: "This announcement is like a dream come true", says Roy Styles. "Never has there been such a beautiful, balanced and perfect looking express passenger locomotive." Greg Tingey has a list of improvements at hand: "better ashpan draughting, bigger drive bearings and rollers on all axles, *Duke of Gloucester*-type poppet valves." Another, Steve Glover, has "completed a four-year build of a 3½" gauge (54in long) working steam model of 'P2' No. 2006 *Wolf of Badenoch*, the last one built. I have offered the model to the A1 Trust for fundraising." While this is a very generous offer, it is all too easy to see emotions running high as 'P2' factions battle over whether No. 2007 should be streamlined, with the 'A4' nose treatment applied to *Lord President*, *Mons Meg*, *Thane of Fife* and *Wolf of Badenoch*, or shaped in the earlier and supremely elegant style of *Cock o' The North* and *Earl Marischal*. The Trust will make its own decision, but *Cock o' The North* is very likely to be the model for the seventh 'P2'.

As for a name, well this is anyone's guess. Tornado struck exactly the right note. *Holyrood*, *Teribus*, *Maid of Norway* and *Sir Walter Scott* have been suggested, but none of these quite lives up to the picture of the locomotives O. S. Nock painted above, nor to the sheer beauty of line of *Cock o' The North*. As of late 2010, however, the 'P2' is still very much a proposal. As Mark Allatt says, "The aim of the study is to answer the question once and for all as to whether the Trust can successfully build, certify and operate a 'P2'. If the answer is yes, then we will launch the project. If no, then we will look at an alternative locomotive to build. Anyone wishing to play a part in this exciting adventure should come on board as one of our convenators if they are not already."

Quite what an alternative locomotive might be is anyone's shout. If, ultimately, a 'P2' is really out of the question, a Gresley 4-8-2 can only be the haziest wisp of a pipedream. A Thompson 'A2/2', though, would be beyond the pale.

Another Peppercorn 'A1' anyone, or how about two?

The crest on *Tornado's* distinctive nameplate is that of RAF Cottesmore – motto 'We rise to our obstacles'. Below it is a plaque commemorating *Tornado's* naming by Their Royal Highnesses the Prince of Wales and the Duchess of Cornwall on 19th February 2009.
MATT HOWELL

'A1' CLASS PACIFIC

Introduced 1948
Tornado   2008

	Imperial	Metric
Wheel arrangement	4-6-2	2-3-1
Length over buffers (including tender)	72ft 11¾in	22.22m
Maximum height (original 'A1')	13ft 1in	3.99m
Maximum height (*Tornado*)	13ft 0in	3.99m
Maximum width (over cab side screens)	9ft 2⅞in	2.82m
Total locomotive and tender weight (full)	166 tons 2cwt	168.8 tonnes
Weight of locomotive only (full)	105 tons 4cwt	106.9 tonnes
Adhesive weight (full boiler)	66 tons 11cwt	67.7 tonnes
Maximum axle load	22 tons 7cwt	22.7 tonnes
Boiler pressure (maximum)	250lb/sq in	17.25 bar
Nominal tractive effort @ 85% boiler pressure	37,397lb	168.38kN
Maximum speed	100mph	160km/h
Current certified top speed	75mph	120km/h
Driving wheel diameter	6ft 8in	2.03m
Bogie wheel diameter	3ft 2in	0.97m
Trailing carrying wheel diameter	3ft 8in	1.12m
Cylinders	3	3
Piston stroke	26in	660mm
Piston diameter	19in	480mm
Valves	Inside admission piston type	
Valve diameter	10in	0.25m
Valve gear	Walschaerts (3 sets)	
Exhaust system	Double choke Kylala Chapelon (Kylchap)	
Axle bearings	Timken taper roller throughout	

BOILER

Type (original 'A1')	Diagram 118 (LNER)	
Type (*Tornado*)	Diagram 118A (LNER/Meiningen)	

	Imperial	Metric
Maximum diameter	6ft 5in	1.96m
Overall length	29ft 2in	8.89m
Distance between tube plates	16ft 11⅝in	5.17m
Heating surface (firebox)	245.30sq ft	22.79m²
Heating surface (small tubes)	1211.57sq ft	112.56m²
Heating surface (superheater flue tubes)	1004.50sq ft	93.32m²
Total evaporative heating surface	2461.37sq ft	228.67m²
Superheater heating surface	697.67sq ft	64.12m²
Grand total heating surface	3141.04sq ft	291.81m²
Firebox	Wide (Wooton) type with combustion chamber (copper); *Tornado* (steel)	
Grate area	50sq ft	4.65m²
Grate type	Rocking with hopper ashpan	
Small tubes (diameter)	121 × 2¼in	57.2mm
Superheater flues	43 × 4 pass elements	

TENDER

	Imperial	Metric
Wheel arrangement	8 wheels, rigid frame	
Weight (full)	60 tons 18cwt	61.87 tonnes
Coal capacity (original 'A1')	9 tons	9.4 tonnes
Coal capacity (*Tornado*)	7.5 tons	7.7 tonnes
Water capacity (original 'A1')	5000 gallons	22700 litres
Water capacity (*Tornado*)	6200 gallons	28200 litres
Wheel diameter	4ft 2in	1.27m

THE 'A1' LOCOMOTIVE FLEET

No.	Name	Built at	To traffic	First shed	Final shed	Boilers
60113	Great Northern	Doncaster	25/9/45	Doncaster	Doncaster (1957)	New/60016/60016/60002/60015
60114	W. P. Allen	Doncaster	6/8/48	King's Cross	Doncaster (1957)	New/60156/60538/60148/60144/60125/60115/60123
60115	Meg Merrilies	Doncaster	3/9/48	Gateshead	Copley Hill (1960)	New/60114/60505/60149/60131/60149
60116	Hal O'The Wynd	Doncaster	8/10/48	Heaton	Gateshead (1964)	New/60530/60130/60148/60143/60151
60117	Bois Roussel	Doncaster	22/10/48	Grantham	Ardsley (1965)	New/60530/60130/60148/60143/60151
60118	Archibald Sturrock	Doncaster	12/11/48	Copley Hill	Neville Hill (1963)	New/60147/new/60152/new
60119	Patrick Stirling	Doncaster	26/11/48	Copley Hill	Doncaster (1958)	New/60151/60146/60147/60533/60157
60120	Kittiwake	Doncaster	10/12/48	King's Cross	York (1963)	New/60533/60130/new
60121	Silurian	Doncaster	22/12/48	York throughout		New/60146/60136/60129/60139/60116/60124
60122	Curlew	Doncaster	24/12/48	King's Cross	Doncaster (1959)	New/60527/60116/60162/60136/60150/60156
60123	H. A. Ivatt	Doncaster	10/2/49	Doncaster	Ardsley (1962)	New/60126/60535/60155/60127
60124	Kenilworth	Doncaster	23/3/49	Gateshead	Darlington (1964)	New/60138/60139/60135/60152/60136/60152/60145
60125	Scottish Union	Doncaster	22/4/49	Doncaster	Doncaster (1958)	New/60154/new/60124/60530/60128/60161
60126	Sir Vincent Raven	Doncaster	27/4/49	Heaton	York (1961)	New/60131/60531/60505/60137/60118/new
60127	Wilson Worsdell	Doncaster	13/5/49	Heaton	Gateshead (1964)	New/60140/60144/60151/60519/60141/60537
60128	Bongrace	Doncaster	19/5/49	Copley Hill	Doncaster (1959)	New/new/60123/new/60146/60155/60134/60146
60129	Guy Mannering	Doncaster	15/6/49	York	York (1965)	New/60128/60143/60145/60531/60518/60158/60534/60155
60130	Kestrel	Darlington	28/9/48	Doncaster	Ardsley (1964)	New/60511/60525/60119/60142/60159/60151
60131	Osprey	Darlington	5/10/48	King's Cross	Neville Hill (1963)	New/60158/60125/60123/60129
60132	Marmion	Darlington	18/10/48	Gateshead	Gateshead (1964)	New/60145/60129/60138/60533/60525/60156/60158
60133	Pommern	Darlington	30/10/48	Grantham	Ardsley (1954)	New/60155/60143/60132/60151
60134	Foxhunter	Darlington	5/11/48	Copley Hill	Neville Hill (1963)	New/60155/60537/60121/60532
60135	Madge Wildfire	Darlington	18/11/48	Gateshead	Ardsley (1962)	New/60138/60152/60515/60127/60128/60501/60125
60136	Alcazar	Darlington	26/11/48	Copley Hill	Doncaster (1959)	New/60162/60539/60133/60144/60514
60137	Redgauntlet	Darlington	3/12/48	Gateshead	Tweedmouth (1962)	New/60532/60515/60160/60120/60125/60135/60123
60138	Boswell	Darlington	10/12/48	York throughout		New/60143/60132/60526/60537/60154/60162/60525
60139	Sea Eagle	Darlington	23/12/48	King's Cross	Doncaster (1959)	New/60149/60117/60129/60115/60505/60125
60140	Balmoral	Darlington	24/12/48	York	York (1950)	New/60144/60531/60118/60156/60131/60119
60141	Abbotsford	Darlington	31/12/48	York	York (1963)	New/60137/60128/60143/60138/60133/new
60142	Edward Fletcher	Darlington	2/2/49	Gateshead	Gateshead (1964)	New/60135/60128/60161/60127/60129
60143	Sir Walter Scott	Darlington	22/2/49	Gateshead	York (1963)	New/60127/60130/60131/60125/60152/60139/60506/60157
60144	King's Courier	Darlington	2/3/49	Doncaster	Doncaster (1957)	New/60139/60533/60155/60116/60145/60114
60145	Saint Mungo	Darlington	23/3/49	Gateshead	York (1964)	New/60121/60501/60122/60126/60515/60501/spare
60146	Peregrine	Darlington	11/4/49	Doncaster	York (1963)	New/60140/60157/60130/60148/60519/60118
60147	North Eastern	Darlington	13/4/49	Gateshead	York (1963)	New/60539/60141/60161/60162/60142/60141
60148	Aboyeur	Darlington	25/5/49	Grantham	Ardsley (1965)	New/60133/60155/new/60115/60116/60153
60149	Amadis	Darlington	31/5/49	Grantham	Doncaster (1961)	New/60142/60531/60148/60519/60150/60124/60536/60147
60150	Willbrook	Darlington	15/6/49	Heaton	York (1960)	New/60124/60156/60140/60538/60142
60151	Midlothian	Darlington	30/6/49	Gateshead	York (1965)	New/60138/60118/60126/60147/60146/60139/60527
60152	Holyrood	Darlington	8/7/49	Haymarket	York (1964)	New/60161/60137/60528/60511/60117/60114
60153	Flamboyant	Doncaster	26/8/49	York throughout		New/60518/60121/60132
60154	Bon Accord	Doncaster	23/9/49	Gateshead	Neville Hill (1963)	New/60154/60156/60513/60114/60159/60160/60116
60155	Borderer	Doncaster	29/9/49	Gateshead	York (1962)	New/new/60150/60511/60156/60513/60511/60515/spare
60156	Great Central	Doncaster	19/10/49	King's Cross	York (1964)	New/60151/60119/60528/60154/60129/60124/60506
60157	Great Eastern	Doncaster	3/11/49	King's Cross	Doncaster (1959)	New/60142/60147/60528/60528/60160
60158	Aberdonian	Doncaster	17/11/49	King's Cross	Doncaster (1958)	New/60125/60539/60114/60141/60126/60137/60533
60159	Bonnie Dundee	Doncaster	24/11/49	Haymarket	St Margarets (1963)	New/60122/60152/60506/60128/60146
60160	Auld Reekie	Doncaster	2/12/49	Haymarket	St Margarets (1963)	New/60530/60153/60137/60140/60120
60161	North British	Doncaster	19/12/49	Haymarket	St Margarets (1963)	New/60149/60135/60159/60122/60160/60521
60162	Saint Johnstoun	Doncaster	23/12/49	Haymarket	St Margarets (1963)	New/60528/60158/60135/60154/60122/60122
60163	Tornado	Darlington	2/8/08	Darlington	-	New

BR Blue	BR Green	Withdrawn	Disposal
1/50	8/52	19/11/62	Doncaster Works
11/49	8/52	26/12/64	Hughes Bolckow, Blyth
6/50	9/52	12/11/62	Doncaster Works
3/50	8/52	14/6/65	Hughes Bolckow, Blyth
7/50	11/51	21/6/65	Clayton & Davie, Dunston
5/50	1/52	4/10/65	T. W. Ward, Beighton
6/50	2/52	31/5/64	Cox & Danks, Wadsley Bridge
3/50	10/51	20/1/64	Darlington Works
5/50	12/51	4/10/65	T. W. Ward, Killamarsh
5/50	10/52	17/12/62	Doncaster Works
12/49	12/52	1/10/62	Doncaster Works
8/50	12/51	27/3/66	A. Draper, Hull
1/51	10/52	4/7/64	Cox & Danks, Wadsley Bridge
7/50	10/51	18/1/65	A. Draper, Hull
New	3/52	14/6/65	Hughes Bolckow, Blyth
New	2/52	10/1/65	A. Draper, Hull
New	2/52	11/10/65	R. A. King, Norwich
7/50	1/52	4/10/65	J. Cashmore, Great Bridge
6/50	9/51	4/10/65	T. W Ward, Killamarsh
11/49	3/52	14/6/65	Hughes Bolckow, Blyth
4/50	6/52	21/6/65	Clayton & Davie, Dunston
3/50	2/53	4/10/65	T. W. Ward, Beighton
10/50	12/52	12/11/62	Doncaster Works
12/50	1/52	22/5/63	Doncaster Works
6/50	3/53	29/10/62	Doncaster Works
9/49	4/52	4/10/65	T. W. Ward, Killamarsh
5/50	9/51	7/6/64	Cox & Danks, Wadsley Bridge
7/50	11/51	11/1/65	A. Draper, Hull
5/50	9/51	5/10/64	A. Draper, Hull
10/50	12/51	14/6/65	Hughes Bolckow, Blyth
9/50	10/51	6/5/64	A. Draper, Hull
1/51	10/51	30/4/63	Doncaster Works
8/50	1/52	19/6/66	A. Draper, Hull
12/50	12/51	4/10/65	T. W. Ward, Killamarsh
11/50	8/51	28/8/64	A. Draper, Hull
1/51	7/52	21/6/65	Arnott Young, Dinsdale
10/50	8/51	7/6/64	Cox & Danks, Wadsley Bridge
1/51	3/52	5/10/64	A. Draper, Hull
3/51	6/52	24/11/65	Station Steel, Wath
6/51	11/52	21/6/65	J. Cashmore, Great Bridge
New	12/51	2/11/62	Doncaster Works
New	8/52	4/10/65	T. W. Ward, Beighton
New	5/52	4/10/65	T. W. Ward, Killamarsh
New	7/52	10/5/65	Clayton & Davie, Dunston
New	11/51	10/1/65	A. Draper, Hull
New	11/52	26/12/64	Hughes Bolckow, Blyth
New	12/52	14/10/63	Inverurie Works
New	3/53	12/12/63	Darlington Works
New	11/52	14/10/63	Inverurie Works
New	8/51	28/10/63	Inverurie Works

Penultimate 'A1' No. 60161 *North British* is undergoing maintenance at its home shed of Haymarket (Edinburgh) in June 1962; despite looking smart, it only has only another 20 months to run. Alongside it is shedmate 'A4' No. 60009 *Union of South Africa*, happily rescued by John Cameron and still running on the main line today.
GEOFF RIXON

FOOTNOTE

The boilers fitted to the 'A1s' when new were to LNER design Diagram 118, and identical to and fully interchangeable with those fitted to Peppercorn 'A2s'. A total of 25 new boilers were constructed after 1950, the last four not being fitted until 1961; an immense waste as it did little to extend the life of the locomotives that carried them. Boiler No. 29880 went to 60118, No. 29882 to 60126, No. 29883 to 60141, while the last one of all, No. 29881 to 60120 (installed in August 1961) had the shortest life as the engine was scrapped after sustaining severe accident damage at Otterington in January 1964.

WHAT'S IN A NAME?

The names of the Peppercorn 'A1s' appear to make a shambolic list. Most people, railwaymen included, heartily agree that they are. The awarding of steam locomotives with a personal identity, almost a human one, goes back to the birth of the railways in 1825 – numbers began to be applied much later – but the idea had run out of energy at the end of the Second World War.

This was the case with the LNER, who had moved from romantic names to honouring its top 'day job' officials, otherwise unknown outside the boardroom. But for their fame on streamlined 'A4s', who otherwise would have heard of Sir Murrough Wilson, Andrew K. McCosh or Walter K. Whigham?

When the production 'A1s' appeared, it was decided at that only first-built No. 60114 would be named. A Labour government was in power at that time, so the honour fell to W. P. [Bill] Allen, a trade union official. *The London Evening Standard* compounded the gloom early in 1949 when one of its columnists suggested that the socialist-led Railway Executive might go further by removing plates from existing engines.

In late 1949, Surrey photographer and enthusiast John Faulkner wrote to the Railway Executive in protest, and by the end of the year it had been agreed to honour the entire fleet, using ideas sent in. Three engines were to follow old LNER policy and commemorate racing winners, along with locomotive designers of pre-1923 railway companies, scrapped North British engines, and finally six bird names displaced from streamlined 'A4s'.

Romantic Scottish author Sir Walter Scott, whose novels were plundered for engine names by the North British Railway, provided inspiration for several more 'A1s', and he even got one named after himself. There was one change of mind, and one mistake. *Guillemot* remained on an 'A4' (No. 60020), being replaced with *Kittiwake*, and No. 60137's plates were originally cast as two words, *Red Gauntlet* — an error soon rectified.

F COULTON

MATT HOWELL

> ## LIVERIES
> Nos. 60114-26, from Doncaster, were delivered in full LNER apple green livery, as were Nos. 60130-52 from Darlington with British Railways lettered in full on the tender. Nos. 60127-9 from Doncaster appeared in blue, with the new 'cycling lion' emblem on the tender.
>
> After the final batch of ten, Nos. 60153-62, appeared from Doncaster in blue, a decision was made to turn them out in Brunswick green, a process starting in August 1951 and lasting until the demise of the class.
>
> New 'A1' No. 60163 *Tornado* uniquely entered service in August 2008 in all-over works grey primer, and was the first main line steam locomotive to carry a website address on its tender. LNER apple green is the A1 Steam Locomotive Trust's preferred 'standard', but other colours will be carried over time, including blue and BR Brunswick green.

60113 *Great Northern* (from new):
Inherited from Gresley Class 'A1' No. 4470

60114 *W. P. Allen* (from 10/48):
Trade union member of Railway Executive

60115 *Meg Merrilies* (from 6/50):
Character in Sir Walter Scott novel

60116 *Hal O'The Wynd* (from 5/51):
Character in Sir Walter Scott novel

60117 *Bois Roussel* (from 7/50):
1938 Derby winner

60118 *Archibald Sturrock* (from 7/50):
GNR chief engineer

60119 *Patrick Stirling* (from 7/50):
GNR chief engineer

60120 *Kittiwake* (from 5/50):
Sea gull

60121 *Silurian* (from 5/50):
1923 Doncaster Cup winner

60122 *Curlew* (by 7/50):
Curved bill marsh bird

60123 *H. A. Ivatt* (from 7/50):
GNR chief engineer

60124 *Kenilworth* (from 8/50):
Character in Sir Walter Scott novel

60125 *Scottish Union* (from 1/51):
1938 St Leger winner

60126 *Sir Vincent Raven:* (from 7/50)
NER chief engineer

60127 *Wilson Worsdell* (from 10/50):
NER chief engineer

60128 *Bongrace* (from 11/50):
1926 Doncaster Cup winner

60129 *Guy Mannering* (from 11/50):
Character in Sir Walter Scott novel

60130 *Kestrel* (from 7/50):
Hunting bird

60131 *Osprey* (from 6/50):
Fish-eating bird of prey

60132 *Marmion* (from 12/50):
Character in Sir Walter Scott novel

60133 *Pommern* (from 4/50):
1915 Derby, 2000 Guineas and St Leger winner

60134 *Foxhunter* (from 10/50):
1932 Doncaster Cup winner

60135 *Madge Wildfire* (from 10/50):
Character in Sir Walter Scott novel

60136 *Alcazar* (from 12/50):
1934 Doncaster Cup winner

60137 *Red Gauntlet/Redgauntlet* (from 6/50):
Character in Sir Walter Scott novel

60138 *Boswell* (from 9/50):
1934 St Leger winner

60139 *Sea Eagle* (from 5/50):
Bird of prey

60140 *Balmoral* (from 7/50):
Scottish Royal stately home

60141 *Abbotsford* (from 5/50):
Home of Sir Walter Scott

60142 *Edward Fletcher* (from 10/50):
NER chief engineer

60143 *Sir Walter Scott* (from 9/50):
Scottish romantic author

60144 *King's Courier* (from 1/51):
1900 Doncaster Cup winner

60145 *Saint Mungo* (from 8/50):
Sobriquet for Glasgow

60146 *Peregrine* (from 12/50):
Bird of prey

60147 *North Eastern* (from 3/52):
Pre-grouping company

60148 *Aboyeur* (from 1/51):
1932 Derby winner

60149 *Amadis* (from 12/50):
1909 Doncaster Cup winner

60150 *Willbrook* (from 1/51):
1914 Doncaster Cup winner

60151 *Midlothian* (from 3/51):
Scottish region

60152 *Holyrood* (from 6/51):
Edinburgh stately house

60153 *Flamboyant* (from 8/50):
1921 Doncaster Cup winner

60154 *Bon Accord* (from 4/51):
Aberdeen motto

60155 *Borderer* (from 3/51):
Scottish borders native

60156 *Great Central* (from 7/52):
Pre-grouping company

60157 *Great Eastern* (from 11/51):
Pre-grouping company

60158 *Aberdonian* (from 3/51):
Aberdeen native

60159 *Bonnie Dundee* (from 7/51):
Character in Sir Walter Scott novel

60160 *Auld Reekie* (from 3/51):
Sobriquet for Edinburgh

60161 *North British* (from 6/51):
Pre-grouping company

60162 *Saint Johnstoun* (from 8/51):
Old name for Perth

60163 *Tornado* (from 2/09):
Jet fighter aircraft

BRIEF LIVES: THE STORY OF THE PIONEER PEPPERCORN 'A1'

First-built 'A1' No. 60114 *W. P. Allen*, arriving at King's Cross with a train from Newcastle on 19th September 1953, is already carrying its second boiler, which was built for sister No. 60156 *Great Central*.
GEOFF RIXON

By the time the first production 'A1' emerged from Doncaster Works in August 1948, all the sparkle had already gone out of celebrating the arrival of new types. This is therefore the story of an everyday engine. While Tornado is the celebrated 50th 'A1', this is an account of the very first of the class, which rolled out of Doncaster almost unnoticed over half a century ago.

No. 60114 did not carry a nameplate at first, although the authorities relented and christened her not after a bird or a racehorse, but W. P. (Bill) Allen, the drivers union's representative on the Railway Executive. The initial livery selected was LNER apple green – as carried by No. 60163 *Tornado* – although this soon gave way to more sombre colours.

The following working history of No. 60114 is credited to Tommy Knox, whose copious notes have been formatted by Phil Champion of the A1 Steam Locomotive Trust.

The first recorded sighting of *W. P. Allen* in service was on 9th August 1948 at Doncaster shed. She appeared in Leeds Central station six days later, working to London on the 2.40pm Leeds-King's Cross on the 18th and the 5.50pm King's Cross-Hull goods on the 20th. She made three brief visits to works for rectification before assignment to regular duties, and was named at King's Cross on 28th October. No. 60114 was regularly used on the 1.30pm King's Cross-Doncaster.

Her outward appearance quickly altered. Within a year, it had been decided the entire class should be repainted in a deep shade of blue, but this idea was quickly discarded and from summer 1951 the policy was to apply Brunswick green, the house colours of the old Great Western. The only noticeable physical changes were the addition of a lip to the chimney, and the lowering of the smokebox door numberplate to allow the lamps to be repositioned.

A transfer to Copley Hill shed (Leeds) took place on 4th June 1950, and No. 60114's new duties included Harrogate-London expresses. She was reallocated to Grantham on 15th February 1953, for a range of East Coast work that included regular trips to Newcastle. Doncaster shed took her over from 2nd September 1957 until withdrawal, widening her sphere of operation to Hull and Leeds. Blackpool was an unusual destination for the 'A1' on 29th July 1961 on a Gainsborough Model Railway Society special, and Worcester was reached on 7th July 1964.

As Knox recalls, *W. P. Allen's* final recorded passenger train was a troop special on 11th September of that year, and her final duty is believed to have been on the 7.33am Aberdeen-King's Cross parcels into York. Ousted by diesels, but with a working life of at least a decade left in her, No. 60114 was laid aside on Boxing Day 1964. The sad engine was dumped at Doncaster shed, and by 3rd March 1965 had been towed to Chater's Bank, Gateshead, leaving six days later on the final trip to Hughes Bolckow's scrapyard in Blyth, Northumberland. The shipbreaker liquidated its arrivals as quickly as possible.

THE A1: A SUM OF MANY PARTS

On a steam locomotive intended for perhaps 50 years, it was likely that every component would be replaced during her lifetime. To reduce time spent in works, it was standard practice to remove parts requiring lengthy overhauls – such as boilers – and install another item that had already been given attention. In time, tenders, even main frames and cabs could be exchanged between engines, with perhaps just nameplates demonstrating true continuity.

In the case of No. 60114 *W. P. Allen*, the 'A1' did not work long enough for the process to run its course, and she certainly ran with the same tender (No. 731) for her entire career, although this particular item was originally intended to go behind last-built 'A2' No. 60539 *Bronzino*.

As will be explained later, the locomotive's original boiler was one of the longest-lived, migrating to another engine every year or so.

No. 60114's visits to works for overhaul

Works	Depot	Work done	In	Out	Boiler No.
Doncaster	King's Cross	Unclassified	24/8/48	26/8/48	9659
Doncaster	King's Cross	Unclassified	6/10/48	13/10/48	9659
Doncaster	King's Cross	Unclassified	18/10/48	26/10/48	9659
Doncaster	King's Cross	Casual Light	4/4/49	28/4/49	9659
Doncaster	King's Cross	General	10/10/49	16/11/49	9659
Doncaster	King's Cross	Weighing	8/3/50	8/3/50	9659
Doncaster	Copley Hill	Casual Light	17/3/50	24/3/50	9659
Doncaster	Copley Hill	Intermediate Heavy	21/2/51	22/3/51	9659/29829
Doncaster	Copley Hill	General	14/7/52	15/8/52	29836
Doncaster	Copley Hill	Casual Light	6/1/53	20/1/53	29836
Grantham	Grantham	Weighing	23/7/53	23/7/53	29836
Doncaster	Grantham	Weigh and adjust	16/3/53	16/3/53	29836
Doncaster	Grantham	General	20/1/54	25/2/54	29806
Doncaster	Grantham	Weighing	24/8/54	24/8/54	29806
Doncaster	Grantham	General	14/6/55	20/7/55	29874
Doncaster	Grantham	Casual Light	13/12/55	22/12/55	29874
Doncaster	Grantham	General	6/3/57	5/4/57	29873
Doncaster	Doncaster	Weighing	22/8/58	22/8/58	29873
Doncaster	Doncaster	General	27/10/58	5/12/58	29814
Doncaster	Doncaster	Casual Light	19/6/59	25/7/59	29814
Doncaster	Doncaster	General	19/5/60	13/7/60	29831
Doncaster	Doncaster	General	17/7/62	19/6/62	29809
Doncaster	Doncaster	Adjustments	24/9/62	27/9/62	29809
Doncaster	Doncaster	Casual Light	13/5/63	12/6/63	29809

ONE BOILER… SIX LOCOMOTIVES

The boiler made for first production 'A1' was coincidentally one of the very longest lived, being employed for almost 17 years on a total of six locomotives (one of them carrying it twice). The official record card states that boiler No. 9659, which was fitted new to No. 60114 when she first rolled out of Doncaster Works in August 1948, spent less than half its life with an 'A1', and from March 1956 migrated to the similar mixed-traffic 'A2'.

Demonstrating how hard the 'A1s' were worked, especially those based at King's Cross top shed, No. 60114 ran 23,878 miles within her first four months – around 1,500 a week, and a feat maintained throughout 1949.

Boiler No. 9659, renumbered 29829 during a general reorganisation of major components in March 1951, was removed from No. 60114's during her general overhaul in July 1952 with 280,319 miles to its credit, and after two months refettling went to the next locomotive needing one – Gateshead's No. 60115 *Meg Merrilies*. This second career was only a short one, because by February 1954 (103,727 miles later), No. 60115 was back at Doncaster for a 'general'. Boiler No. 29829's next home was Heaton's No. 60116 *Hal O' The Wynd*, a relationship that would last until August 1955 and take it 86,748 miles.

That was the end of No. 29829's career with an 'A1', because the next locomotive at Doncaster requiring a replacement boiler was 'A2/3' No. 60534 *Irish Elegance* from Haymarket (Edinburgh). In October 1957, and after 113,014 miles, a switch took place to York regular No. 60512 *Steady Aim*. Some 93,055 miles were then run before No. 29829 passed to York stablemate No. 60522 *Straight Deal* in February 1960. Sadly Doncaster's record card carries no entries beyond this date, logging that the engine only worked some 38,685 miles during this year, raising the total to 715,548.

A final works visit agreed in August 1962 was to be the boiler's salvation for another three years. A sharp reduction in East Coast work for York's Pacifics at the end of the summer season created a dump at Scarborough, from which they never returned.

No. 60512 *Steady Aim* survived because she was in Doncaster Works at the time, being refitted with our trusty and far from rusty boiler No. 29829, and a deal was struck for the locomotive to go to the Scottish Region. No. 60512 eked out her final days with only a brief visit to Cowlairs (Glasgow) in May 1963. No mileage records are available for her duties from St Margaret's (Edinburgh), Polmadie and Dundee sheds, but it can be safely suggested that boiler No. 29829 ran a career total of over 800,000 miles. After withdrawal from service on 19th June 1965, the engine was sent to Motherwell Machinery & Scrap Company for dismantling.

Date	Engine	Class	Miles
10/48-12/48	60114	A1	23878
1949	60114	A1	79865
1950	60114	A1	70303
1951	60114	A1	66586
1/52-8/52	60114	A1	39687
9/52-12/52	60115	A1	27407
1953	60115	A1	76201
1/54	60115	A1	119
2/54-12/54	60116	A1	54652
1955	60116	A1	32096
3/56-12/56	60534	A2	60420
1/57-12/57	60534	A2	52594
12/57	60512	A2	6920
1958	60512	A2	38416
1959	60512	A2	47719
1960	60522	A2	38685*
8/62	60512	A2	

*No mileage records kept at NRM after this date

WHO WAS W.P. ALLEN?

William Philip Allen (11th November 1888-4th May 1958, always known as Bill) was described by railway historian Michael Bonavia as "short and cheerful, with a fine old-fashioned waxed moustache… his approach was friendly and down-to-earth, and he made the move from one side of the negotiating table to the other appear quite effortless."

Allen started his working career as a locomotive cleaner at Hornsey shed in North London, and in 1940 rose to the rank of General Secretary of ASLEF (Associated Society of Locomotive Engineers and Firemen), then one of Britain's most influential trade unions, and became its representative on the nationalised Railway Executive.

His elevation was despised by many anti-management staff who regarded him as a turncoat, and there are unsubstantiated stories that the 'A1' dedicated to him had to be carefully supervised when it arrived on unfamiliar depots as there was a tendency for the nameplates to be removed and thrown aside.

BIBLIOGRAPHY

Allen, Cecil J., *British Pacific Locomotives*, Ian Allan, 1962

Brown F. A. S., *Nigel Gresley – Locomotive Engineer*, Ian Allan, 1961

Bulleid, H. A. V., *Master Builders of Steam*, Ian Allan, 1963

Clay, John F., *Essays in Steam*, Ian Allan, 1970

Cox, E. S., *Locomotive Panorama Volume 2*, Ian Allan, 1966

Nock O. S., *British Locomotives from the Footplate*, Ian Allan, 1950

Nock, O. S., *British Steam Locomotives at Work*, George Allen and Unwin, 1967

Nock, O. S., *Locomotive Practice and Performance, Vol 1: The Age of Steam*, Patrick Stephens Ltd, 1989

RCTS, *Locomotives of the LNER*

Rogers, Colonel H. C. B., *Thompson & Peppercorn: Locomotive Engineers*, Ian Allan, 1979

Rogers, Colonel H. C. B., *Express Steam Locomotive Development in Britain & France*, OPC, 1990

Rogers, Colonel H. C. B., *Transition from Steam*, Ian Allan, 1980

Yeadon, W. B., *Yeadon's Register of LNER Locomotives Vol. 3*, Book Law, 2001

The National Railway Museum Archive

Steam Railway

Steam Railway News

The Railway Magazine

SLS Journal (Stephenson Locomotive Society)

The Engineer

INDEX